Flexible Exchange Rates and International Business

by *John M. Blin,* Senior Vice-President,
New ork Futures Exchange, and Adjunct Professor of Managerial Economics
and Decision Sciences, J.L. Kellogg
Graduate School of Management, Northwestern University

Stuart I. Greenbaum, H.L. Stuart Professor
of Banking and Finance, and Director of
the Banking Research Center, The
Kellogg School

Donald P. Jacobs, Dean, and Gaylord
Freeman Distinguished Professor of
Banking, The Kellogg School

*This report was produced in collaboration with the
J.L. Kellogg Graduate School of Management,
Northwestern University*

BRITISH-NORTH AMERICAN COMMITTEE

Sponsored by
**British-North American Research Association (U.K.)
NPA (U.S.A.)
C.D. Howe Institute (Canada)**

ISBN 0-89068-058-2
Library of Congress Catalog Card Number 81-85396

Published by the British-North American Committee

Printed and bound in Washington, D.C.
December 1981

Contents

The British-North American Committee .... inside
front cover

Statement of the British-North American Committee
to Accompany the Report vi

Members of the Committee Signing the Statement............. vii

Preface xi

FLEXIBLE EXCHANGE RATES AND INTERNATIONAL BUSINESS
by John M. Blin, Stuart I. Greenbaum and
Donald P. Jacobs

Introduction and Summary of Conclusions............... 1
Introduction 1
Summary of Conclusions 3
Coping with Exchange Risk 4
The Role of Regulations 4
The Impact on Markets 6

I. Foreign Exchange: Bretton Woods and Beyond............ 8
Evolving Institutional Arrangements 8
The World of Bretton Woods....................... 8
The Managed Float................................ 11
The Role of the MNC 13
The Regulatory Framework......................... 22
The Problem of Foreign Exchange Risk................... 26
Problem Statement 26
Transaction Versus Translation Exposure 28
Economic Exposure............................... 29

II. A Survey of International Business Behavior 31
Approach... 31
Issues Addressed.................................... 34
Findings.. 34
Defining and Measuring Exchange Risk 34
Objectives and Strategies of
Foreign Exchange Risk Management 35
Organizational Responses 35
Internal Exchange Risk Control 37
Short-Term Market Hedging Strategies:
Forward and Money Markets...................... 40
Long-Term Hedging Strategies...................... 42
Decisionmaking Processes for Risk Management........ 44
Effects on Asset Management: Inventories
and Direct Foreign Investment 44

III. An Appraisal of Corporate Behavior
and Public Policy Implications 46
  Hedging: Prudent Management or
    Illusory Insurance?.............................. 46
    The Case for Selective Hedging 46
    Regulations...................................... 47
  Foreign Exchange Markets' Performance and
    International Capital Market Integration 48
    Impact on Foreign Exchange Markets 48
    Risk Bearing, Risk Shifting and Interest-Rate
      Arbitrage 49
    Macro Adjustments: Cause or Effect 52
  Beyond Market Adjustments: Corporate Structure
    and Function.................................... 56
    Markets Versus Corporate Structure 56
    The Firm's Capital Structure
      as a Hedging Vehicle 57
    Asset Structure.................................. 59
    Organizational Adjustments 61
    Improving Risk Management 62

Appendix 1:   **The Questionnaire**.......................... 64

Appendix 2:   **Responses to the Questionnaire** 68

Appendix 3:   **Annualized Monthly Percentage Changes of**
                    Major Exchange Rates, 1972–80. 91

Members of the British-North American Committee 93

Sponsoring Organizations 98

Publications of the British-North American Committee .... inside
                                                                  back cover

Tables

Table 1: Average Annualized Monthly Percentage
           Changes of Major Exchange Rates, 1972–80 (U.S.\$
           against Pound and Deutsche Mark)................. 15
Table 2: U.S.\$ against Swiss Franc and Yen 17
Table 3: Pound against Deutsche Mark, Swiss Franc and Yen 19
Table 4: Deutsche Mark against Swiss Franc and Yen;
           Swiss Franc against Yen 21
Table 5: Balance Sheet, Subsidiary X Ltd. 26
Table 6: Measuring Translation Exposure
           for Subsidiary X Ltd. 28

Table 7: Companies and Other Organizations Interviewed....... 32
Table 8: Autocorrelation Coefficients of Annualized
Month-to-Month Changes in Exchange-Rate
Movements and International Interest-Rate
Differentials...................................... 51
Table 9: Reserve Use and the Exchange-Rate Regime.......... 54

Charts

Chart 1: Monthly Exchange-Rate Movements, 1972–80
(Pound and Deutsche Mark per Dollar).............. 14
Chart 2: Swiss Franc and Yen per Dollar.................... 16
Chart 3: Deutsche Mark, Yen and Swiss Franc per Pound...... 18
Chart 4: Swiss Franc and Yen per Deutsche Mark and
Yen per Swiss Franc 20
Chart 5: Short-Term Interest Rates......................... 59
Chart 6: Euro-Currency Interest Rates...................... 60
Chart 7: Long-Term Interest Rates 61
Chart 8: Differences Between Bond Yields and
Inflation Rates................................... 62

Statement of the British-North American Committee to Accompany the Report

Important new problems were created in the early 1970s when the system of fixed foreign exchange rates established at Bretton Woods broke down and was replaced by flexible rates among the major currencies. For the first time since multinational corporations and financial institutions became significant factors in world trade and investment, their transnational activities were subject to frequent and often major shifts in exchange rates. Multinational business operations today face risks and instabilities unknown under the Bretton Woods system.

Some attention has been paid to how banks and other financial institutions evaluate the operations of foreign exchange markets under these circumstances. However, no systematic study has been made public of how business firms are actually coping from day to day with fluctuating exchange rates, given the differences in regulations and economic conditions among the countries in whose currencies they keep their accounts.

To fill this gap, the British-North American Committee initiated a study of these matters. In collaboration with the J.L. Kellogg Graduate School of Management at Northwestern University, it undertook an assessment of experience and behavior among some important firms and institutions in the United States, United Kingdom and Canada. These firms range from those engaged in extractive, processing and manufacturing activities to those providing various financial services.

The study addresses the following issues.

• How do firms involved in international operations perceive, measure, monitor, and control their foreign exchange risks?
• Who within the company assumes responsibility for foreign exchange decisions?
• What effect have flexible exchange rates had on the organizational structure of firms and on the presentation of their accounts?
• What effect have flexible exchange rates had on pricing, invoicing, inventory management, investment, and financing decisions?

The authors present their findings in Chapter II. In Chapter III, they suggest some policy implications for managing risks under present circumstances.

We are grateful to one of our members, Donald P. Jacobs, Dean of the Kellogg School, for arranging for two members of his faculty, Professors John M. Blin (subsequently appointed Senior Vice President of the New York Futures Exchange) and Stuart I. Greenbaum, to undertake this study. We are also indebted to other committee members who contributed information and helped with the funding of this project.

We are pleased to publish this report, which brings together for the first time certain facts about how the international private sector is adjusting to an important new reality.

Members of the Committee Signing the Statement

ROBERT R. FREDERICK
Executive Vice President, International
Sector, General Electric Company

THEODORE GEIGER
Distinguished Research Professor of In-
tersocietal Relations, School of Foreign
Service, Georgetown University

GWAIN GILLESPIE
Senior Vice President-Finance and Administration, Heublein Inc.

MALCOLM GLENN
Executive Vice President, Reed Holdings,
Incorporated

GEORGE GOYDER
Sudbury, Suffolk

JOHN H. HALE
Executive Vice President, Alcan
Aluminium Limited

HON. HENRY HANKEY
British Secretary, BNAC

AUGUSTIN S. HART, JR.
Director, Quaker Oats Company

G.R. HEFFERNAN
President, Co-Steel International Ltd.

HENRY J. HEINZ II
Chairman of the Board, H.J. Heinz Company

ROBERT HENDERSON
Chairman, Kleinwort Benson Ltd.

HENDRIK S. HOUTHAKKER
Professor of Economics, Harvard University

TOM JACKSON
General Secretary, Union of Communication Workers

DONALD P. JACOBS
Dean, J.L. Kellogg Graduate School of
Management, Northwestern University

JOHN V. JAMES
Chairman of the Board, President and
Chief Executive Officer, Dresser
Industries, Inc.

GEORGE S. JOHNSTON
President, Scudder, Stevens & Clark

JOSEPH D. KEENAN
President, Union Label and Service
Trades Department, AFL-CIO

CURTIS M. KLAERNER
President and Chief Operating Officer,
Commonwealth Oil Refining Company

H.U.A. LAMBERT
Chairman, Barclays Bank International
Ltd.

HERBERT H. LANK
Honorary Director, Du Pont Canada Inc.

WILLIAM A. LIFFERS
Vice Chairman, American Cyanamid
Company

SIR PETER MACADAM
Chairman, B.A.T. Industries Ltd.

RAY W. MACDONALD
Honorary Chairman, Burroughs
Corporation

IAN MacGREGOR
Honorary Chairman, AMAX Inc.

CARGILL MacMILLAN, JR.
Senior Vice President, Cargill Inc.

JOHN D. MACOMBER
Chairman, Celanese Corporation

J.P. MANN
Deputy Chairman, United Biscuits
(Holdings) Ltd.

WILLIAM A. MARQUARD
Chairman, President and Chief Executive
Officer, American Standard Inc.

A.B. MARSHALL
Chairman, Bestobell Ltd.

WILLIAM J. McDONOUGH
Chairman, Asset and Liability Management Committee, The First National Bank
of Chicago

DONALD E. MEADS
Chairman and President, Carver
Associates

SIR PATRICK MEANEY
Group Managing Director, Thomas Tilling
Limited

C.J. MEDBERRY, III
Chairman of the Board, BankAmerica
Corporation and Bank of America NT&SA

SIR PETER MENZIES
Welwyn, Hertfordshire

JOHN MILLER
Vice Chairman and Acting President, NPA

ALLEN E. MURRAY
President of Marketing and Refining Division, Mobil Oil Corporation

KENNETH D. NADEN
President, National Council of Farmer Cooperatives

CONOR CRUISE O'BRIEN
Director, Observer Newspaper Company, Ltd.

WILLIAM S. OGDEN
Vice Chairman, The Chase Manhattan Bank, N.A.

BROUGHTON PIPKIN
Stow-on-the-Wold, Gloucestershire

SIR RICHARD POWELL
Hill Samuel Group Ltd.

ALFRED POWIS
Chairman and President, Noranda Mines Limited

LOUIS PUTZE
Consultant, Rockwell International Corp.

MERLE R. RAWSON
Chairman and Chief Executive Officer, The Hoover Company

CARL E. REICHARDT
President and Director, Wells Fargo Bank

BEN ROBERTS
Professor of Industrial Relations, London School of Economics

HAROLD B. ROSE
Group Economic Advisor, Barclays Bank Limited

DAVID SAINSBURY
Director of Finance, J. Sainsbury Ltd.

WILLIAM SALOMON
Limited Partner and Honorary Member of the Executive Committee, Salomon Brothers

A.C.I. SAMUEL
Handcross, Sussex

NATHANIEL SAMUELS
Chairman, Advisory Board, Lehman Brothers Kuhn Leob Inc., and Chairman, Olivetti Corporation

SIR FRANCIS SANDILANDS
Chairman, Commercial Union Assurance Company, Ltd.

HON. MAURICE SAUVE
Executive Vice President, Administrative and Public Affairs, Consolidated-Bathurst Inc.

PETER F. SCOTT
President, Provincial Insurance Company, Ltd.

ROBERT C. SEAMANS, JR.
Massachusetts Institute of Technology

LORD SEEBOHM
Dedham, Essex

THE EARL OF SELKIRK
President, Royal Central Asian Society

JACOB SHEINKMAN
Secretary-Treasurer, Amalgmated Clothing & Textile Workers' Union

LORD SHERFIELD
Chairman, Raytheon Europe International Company

R. MICHAEL SHIELDS
Managing Director, Associated Newspapers Group Ltd.

GEORGE L. SHINN
Chairman and Chief Executive Officer, The First Boston Corporation

GEORGE P. SHULTZ
Vice Chairman, Bechtel Group of Companies

GORDON R. SIMPSON
Chairman, General Accident Fire and Life Assurance Corporation Ltd.

SIR ROY SISSON
Chairman, Smiths Industries Limited

SIR LESLIE SMITH
Chairman, BOC International

E. NORMAN STAUB
Chairman and Chief Executive Officer, The Northern Trust Company

RALPH I. STRAUS
New York, N.Y.

SIR ROBERT TAYLOR
Deputy Chairman, Standard Chartered Bank Ltd.

WILLIAM I.M. TURNER, JR.
President and Chief Executive Officer,
Consolidated-Bathurst, Inc.

W.O. TWAITS
Toronto, Ontario

MARTHA REDFIELD WALLACE
Director, The Henry Luce Foundation Inc.

GLENN E. WATTS
President, Communications Workers of
America, AFL-CIO

WILLIAM L. WEARLY
Chairman, Executive Committee,
Ingersoll-Rand Company

VISCOUNT WEIR
Vice Chairman, The Weir Group Limited

FREDERICK B. WHITTEMORE
Managing Director, Morgan Stanley &
Co. Incorporated

SIR ERNEST WOODROOFE
Former Chairman, Unilever Ltd.

Preface

We wish to acknowledge the indispensible contributions of the financial officers from those organizations whom we interviewed, listed on page 32, and of the wider group who responded to the questionnaire. We are also indebted to those from within and without the BNAC who commented on early drafts or provided illustrative material from their data banks. Finally, we appreciate the support for this project from the British-North American Committee and the guidance of a special Task Force of its members under the chairmanship of Dirk de Bruyne and William Ogden.

At the same time, we assume sole responsibility for the views and analyses presented here, which do not necessarily represent those of the organizations or individuals referred to above.

John M. Blin
Stuart I. Greenbaum
Donald P. Jacobs

November 1981

Introduction and Summary of Conclusions

INTRODUCTION

Perhaps no single development in the post World War II monetary scene has so challenged the operations of international business as the advent of flexible exchange rates between the world's major currencies.[1] These operations experienced their greatest burst of growth under the Bretton Woods agreement of 1944, which both established fixed exchange rates and committed each of the signatory countries to maintain them by appropriate economic and monetary measures. Although exchange-rate flexibility was sometimes advocated by economists and policymakers during the 1950s and '60s, fixed rates prevailed. This off-stage advice did not interfere with the day-to-day conduct of international business, in which stable currency prices could be relied on. Devaluations were infrequent and revaluations rarer still.

August 1971 marked a turning point in the world monetary system when President Nixon ended the U.S. dollar convertibility into gold at an official fixed price. A few months later, the Smithsonian Agreement attempted to reestablish fixed parities with wider bands of variation and make official the dollar's devaluation. This effort to salvage the system failed, and by March 1973, exchange rates were being determined by market forces. These events were a fitting overture for the torment of an international economy having to adjust to growing inflation, to the relentless escalation of oil prices and to the domestic economic disturbances in every major industrialized country.

Soon after the inception of flexible rates, economists, policymakers and business leaders started looking for proof of earlier assertions about the advantages or disadvantages of floating rates. The record showed sharp daily fluctuations but no clear-cut sign of decline in international trade. As the decade unfolded, more data accumulated. Some of this evidence is easily accessible in public statistical records, but much is difficult to obtain as it pertains to individual corporations dealing in international markets through exports, imports and foreign production facilities. Clearly, our understanding of the effects of flexible ex-

---

1 The terms "flexible" and "floating" exchange rates are used interchangeably throughout the report, although widespread central bank intervention is recognized.

change rates in this period would be greatly improved if we could go beyond traditional macroeconomic studies of exchange-rate adjustments and exchange market efficiency issues to assess the impact of this new situation on corporate behavior.

In late 1978, after more than five years' experience with flexible rates, the British-North American Committee recognized the need for such a study. Its design and conduct were undertaken by a research team from the J.L. Kellogg Graduate School of Management at Northwestern University: Professors John M. Blin, Stuart I. Greenbaum and Dean Donald P. Jacobs, a BNAC member. A preliminary inquiry among the U.S., U.K. and Canadian committee members revealed their willingness to offer their companies' experiences in support of the research. The work began in 1979 with a series of in-depth interviews with major firms in the United States and the United Kingdom, followed by a more broadly based survey questionnaire, which also included a few Canadian companies. Preliminary findings were discussed at BNAC meetings in 1979 and 1980. Before preparing the final report, the authors conferred again with some of the financial officers first interviewed.

Throughout the inquiry, the questions addressed were both strategic and tactical, factual and conceptual. How is foreign exchange risk perceived and measured? How are traditional accounting practices reconciled with today's realities? How are decisions concerning direct investment and those involving operations, inventory management and financing influenced by the risks attendant flexible exchange rates?

The significance of these issues is as great today as at the onset of this study since exchange-rate shifts between major currencies have not diminished. Daily, even hourly, rumors of continued strength for the deutsche mark, softening of the yen, rebounding of the Swiss franc keep surfacing in the media.

The meaning of this depends, of course, on the position of the observer. To the average citizen, exposure to foreign exchange-rate problems may be limited to traveling and shopping abroad. To this person, floating exchange rates are a part of the confusion and uncertainty of the current political and economic world.

To students of international finance, however, the fluctuations among exchange rates are of central interest. They know what the Bretton Woods regime meant in the 1950s and '60s with successive "runs" on the pound, the franc and the mark, yet requiring only an occasional mental readjustment to a new rate between major currencies. Today, such people do not even attempt to keep track of the last two decimals in key rates. And, with an appreciation of the uncertainty and unpredictability of events, they may even admit relief at not having to do business on these stormy seas.

The treasurer of a major corporation—the central actor in this study—lives no such sheltered life, however, being involved with each company purchase of raw materials or components abroad, each sale to foreign clients and indeed in all other foreign operations. The treasurer cannot afford to ignore the realities of "foreign exchange exposure" but must reckon with an accountant whose books are barely recognizable since their last review, rife with seemingly ballooned debts, oddly valued inventories and unrealistically appraised fixed assets. And, even if able to accept the accountant's view of the world, the treasurer still has to explain to a puzzled board why the earnings from such seemingly profitable foreign operations appear to have eroded at the reporting hour.

The saga of the corporate treasurer wrestling with uncooperative, volatile exchange rates and constantly seeking a firm base on which to establish budgets, project cash flows and build financing strategies has now spanned nearly a decade. This report explores the issues involved, the pattern of corporate responses and the implications of these developments in the light of policy issues and economists' recommendations.

SUMMARY OF CONCLUSIONS

The investigations underlying this study can be grouped under three basic questions.

(1) To what extent are firms able to cope with the exchange risk problems to which they are exposed; and how do they actually do this and at what (and at whose) cost?

(2) What roles are played by institutional factors, such as financial reporting regulations, banking and tax legislation and the trading practices of foreign exchange markets?

(3) How do these institutional factors affect financial and goods markets across countries?

Coping with Exchange Risk

The firms interviewed and surveyed for this report—domiciled in the United States, the United Kingdom and Canada—have indeed adapted to the reality of unpredictable exchange rates. They do not appear to have refrained from increasing their direct foreign investment in the face of rate uncertainties. Instances of actual retrenchment are infrequent. Rather, the inquiry found the following responses.

• Firms are attempting to appraise the *economic risk* in exchange-rate fluctuations, often beyond the accountant's financial statements.

• Internal reporting channels, criteria and organizational structures are emerging to monitor and deal with overall exposure. Specific responsibility for these tasks has become better identified, with or without additional staffing and other resources.

• Little impact is acknowledged on pricing or inventory decisions along the lines often suggested by economists, such as lengthening payables in weak currencies. Actual changes in pricing or inventories are reported to be prompted by considerations transcending exchange risk, such as the competitive structure of product markets.

• At the same time, the use of systematic hedging procedures based on markets for deferred delivery of currencies (the so-called forward markets) is widespread and growing.

• Finally, there is consideration of the foreign exchange implications of long-term financing schemes and overall capital structure.

These responses to exchange risk appear to be far less worrisome to corporate policymakers than those often predicted by the flexible exchange-rate critics of the 1960s.

The Role of Regulations

Institutional arrangements in the form of laws and regulations relating to financial reporting, bank practices and taxation shape the responses of firms to exchange risk. The sampled firms are subject to disparate rules governing accounting and financial reporting practices. Indeed, there is little agreement among accounting professionals as to what and how much is "at risk" within a firm's balance sheet and income statement. This sometimes leads firms to adjust for internal planning purposes in appraising their foreign performance. The experience of U.S. firms with the original version of FASB No. 8 illustrates the unsettled state of the debate on accounting for exchange-rate exposure.[2] It should not be surprising, then, that accounting standards and practices differ across national borders and that firms seeking to hedge accounting exposure are found engaging in markedly different practices.

Tax regulations work through a variety of channels. Tax disparities in definitions of gains and losses and in tax rates magnify the problem of managing exposure. For instance, if the need for cover against unfavorable translation of foreign operations is met with forward contracts, the aftertax impact requires a doubling in the size of cover with a 50 percent income tax rate. Although rarely used in the companies surveyed, these translation cover schemes can be costly.

Banking and overall capital market regulations have probably had the most profound impact on foreign exchange risk and its management. Examples from the Euro-currency and Euro-bond markets reveal a varied and complex pattern of interaction. Disparate restrictions on the international flow of capital, coupled with conflicting domestic interest-rate policies and disparate bank regulations, have led to the growth of huge offshore short-term money and capital markets. Interest-rate arbitrage through the conversion of national monies today (spot markets) and at fixed prices tomorrow (forward markets) has further influenced this evolution. The growth of these markets was spurred by the need for private insurance and credit facilities, but their design owes much to the idiosyncrasies of stabilization policy and public regulation in the nation-states they serve. The result is an efficient set of market-based procedures for dealing with foreign exchange risk when internal procedures are insufficient or lacking. This

---

2 In response to numerous criticisms, the Federal Accounting Standards Board has reconsidered the accounting issues. Following comments on a new and quite altered exposure draft (August 1980) proposing different rules for accounting and translation of foreign operations, the FASB has proposed further revisions.

market web, woven ever tighter between countries, may be one of the most striking and significant aspects of the private handling of risk by corporations. The impact of this web and its key connection with foreign exchange risk management cannot be overstated.

The Impact on Markets

The role of offshore markets as a basis for forward pricing of currencies and the layoff of foreign exchange risk by banks is decisive. When facing foreign exchange risk, a company may decide, as mentioned earlier, to sell (or buy) its foreign currency receivables (payables) at a known price today for delivery in the future, for instance 90 days hence. Economics textbooks usually explain that the buying and selling of these forward contracts by speculators, augmented by arbitrageurs, create forward markets for insuring price risk otherwise borne by firms in their daily transactions involving foreign currencies. However, forward markets are of limited depth. For example, commitments up to six months are readily obtainable whereas forward contracts beyond a year are less actively traded and therefore involve substantial transactions cost. In addition, forward markets involve only a few currencies, and the large commercial banks that dominate such markets seldom assume substantial exchange risk, functioning instead as credit and insurance brokers. By so doing, these banks seek to avoid exchange-rate risk and simply "swap" into or out of a currency by simultaneously buying (or selling) spot and selling (or buying) forward, investing in the Euro-market for this currency during the interim.

This risk-avoiding behavior of banks, coupled with the huge size of the Euro-markets relative to the foreign exchange forward markets, effectively makes the forward premium or discount quoted on major currencies equal to the interest-rate differential between Euro-deposits in these currencies. This contrasts with the traditional view that forward markets and forward prices are determined by a balance between many highly capitalized large speculators acting independently of each other and some world class corporate hedgers and arbitrageurs. Put another way, the so-called forward currency markets are essentially "interest-parity markets" and nothing more. But they are also nothing less, for without the ability to lay off through swaps via the Euro-deposit markets, it is most unlikely that many banks would be willing to assume large open forward positions for even short periods. To be sure, forward currency markets existed before the Euro-currency market emerged. But their explosive growth cannot be disassociated from that of the Euro-market. In other words, risk shifting away from the corporation has necessitated an unhindered growth in the offshore money market for interest-rate arbitrage.

Autonomous hedging transactions can trigger intense market activity as banks lay off their risks and the market searches for traders with complementary hedging needs or speculators willing to absorb some of the exposure. It is difficult to overstate the importance of these markets in dissipating the stress imposed by flexible exchange rates on multinational corporations and the banks that serve them. Such markets are central to risk shifting by corporations. Since the objects of trade are fungible, the markets are portable. Nevertheless, the success of the flexible exchange-rate system probably is critically linked to the innovative vitality of these markets. They may, therefore, require the public regulator's benign neglect.

I. Foreign Exchange: Bretton Woods and Beyond

The significance of floating exchange rates for international trade and finance in the post-1973 period remains debatable. The optimism of early supporters has been tempered by unanticipated exchange-rate volatility and tenacious balance-of-payments disequilibria. Predictions of chaos and despair have also proved unfounded. Markets have developed to shift and dissipate the new private-sector risks, and if these markets occasionally falter, they nevertheless continue to function. Despite justifications that often seem obscure, central banks have felt a need for continued intervention in the exchange market, giving rise to the "managed" or "dirty" float. In this more uncertain milieu, managers face the ever-present need to plan for exchange-rate variability in establishing budgets, projecting cash flows and earnings and formulating business plans. Over eight years of experience with floating rates has generated evidence that warrants careful examination.

In the following discussion, we will describe the development of the present exchange-rate system and the accounting, bank and tax regulations in the United States, the United Kingdom and Canada since Bretton Woods.

EVOLVING INSTITUTIONAL ARRANGEMENTS

The World of Bretton Woods

In July 1944, an international conference was held at Bretton Woods to promote postwar international monetary cooperation. It led to the establishment of a fixed exchange-rate system. With occasional minor modifications, this system endured for almost three decades. The conference's overwhelming resolve was to avoid the myopic errors made after World War I. The memory of the 1930s, when floating exchange rates were associated with paralysis in international trade and finance, protectionist and beggar-thy-neighbor policies, remained vivid. As advisor to the British delegation, Lord Keynes advocated complete demonetization of gold (this "Barbarian relic!") and creation of a world central bank along with a common international reserve asset (the "Bancor"), to be backed by contributions of the member countries' central banks. Exchange parities were to be adjustable in terms of the common reserve asset.

The conference led to the establishment of a pivotal international monetary asset, but the U.S. dollar, rather than an arbitrary bookkeeping construct, was chosen. The role of gold was ostensibly diminished as each currency value was fixed in terms of the dollar. Yet the dollar was freely convertible into gold at $35 an ounce. Thus revived, the gold exchange standard was to endure until August 15, 1971, when President Nixon officially suspended convertibility of the dollar. Subsequent dollar devaluations led to the final abandonment of fixed parities in March 1973. The present system of "managed floating" had been born.

Exchange rates remained stable *vis-à-vis* the dollar for extended periods from 1944 to 1971, despite occasional devaluations and revaluations, sanctioned by the International Monetary Fund, to correct "fundamental balance-of-payments disequilibria."

After sterling was devalued from U.S. $4.00 to $2.80 per pound in 1949, its new parity remained intact for 18 years. Not until 1967 was it again devalued, to $2.40 per pound. Although sterling suffered occasional "runs," variations were limited to a band of ±3/4 percent around the official parity. Intervention usually involved spot purchases or sales of foreign exchange using international reserves or reciprocal central bank credit lines ("swaps"). Stability was occasionally jeopardized as trade and capital flows between countries became unbalanced. As inflation and interest rates diverged among countries, disequilibria became more pronounced and intervention became increasingly compelling. In the words of a central banker, "the drinks were on the house," as speculators, awaiting the virtually assured official exchange-rate adjustment, adopted positions in the pressured currency. This produced occasional spurts of activity in both spot and forward exchange markets, followed by the ultimate devaluation (or revaluation).

Revaluations were less common than devaluations because surplus countries could simply accumulate reserves. A deficit country, on the other hand, had to finance its deficit by borrowing or drawing down reserves. During most of the 1960s, the U.S. balance-of-payments deficits mitigated the liquidity pressures facing most of its trading partners in that the dollar outflow augmented international reserves. As its balance-of-payments deficits continued to mount, the United States confronted the choice of either increasing the dollar price of gold or suspending convertibility. The latter choice in August 1971 signaled the demise of the Bretton Woods fixed exchange-rate system.

During the Bretton Woods period, the adjustments imposed on countries with balance-of-payments deficits often had major political repercussions. Borrowing from other central banks or the IMF frequently necessitated unpopular foreign exchange controls and other domestic monetary measures. Thus, fixed exchange rates involved considerable political exposure, a risk probably most visible in the case of sterling, which was under frequent pressure throughout the 1960s, especially from 1963 to 1967. Pressure on sterling and the periodic need for devaluation became significant political issues as the fixity of rates focused popular attention on exchange-rate policy. Deficit-prone countries, such as France and Italy, displayed similar political sensitivity to exchange-rate developments. Germany and Japan, the major surplus-prone countries, were under less domestic pressure. However, external pressures, especially from the United States, were clearly evident. Established exchange-rate parities became norms to be defended by the ruling political party. A devaluation was an admission of profligacy, whereas a revaluation was popularly interpreted as a sign of weakness, as the surplus country was being forced to accept the adjustment cost on behalf of its less disciplined trading partners. Exchange-rate parity adjustments in either direction were viewed as politically onerous.

In contrast, foreign exchange risk was not a major concern for most private transactors since currency stability was interrupted infrequently; several years often passed without parity adjustments. Currency-related business strategies focused on exchange or capital controls. Forward markets were used selectively as rumors of impending exchange-rate changes spread. The umbrella of central bank intervention was a form of social insurance. Costs of the fixed exchange-rate system were measured in terms of the monetary reserves necessary to support the official parity and distortions in resource allocation due to the occasionally protracted maintenance of disequilibrium exchange rates. Although these costs are not readily measurable, examining managerial resource commitments and exchange-rate volatility under the two regimes represents a plausible first step.

The Managed Float

The unilateral U.S. dollar devaluation in August 1971 was sanctioned by the December 1971 Smithsonian Agreement. This more flexible yet controlled exchange-rate system proved less than durable and collapsed in March 1973. To widespread applause, flexible exchange rates inherited the day.

The new environment surprised many experts. Daily variations in spot and forward exchange rates exceeded expectations even when central banks intervened in the financial markets to maintain orderly conditions. Widely disparate inflation rates developed in Western Europe, North America and Japan. The cartelization of oil prices in late 1973 proved especially destabilizing to the U.S. dollar because of the dollar oil pricing convention. The apparently lethargic reactions of U.S. capital markets to higher inflation rates depressed inflation-adjusted returns on long-term U.S. fixed-income securities relative to those available in West Germany, Switzerland and Japan. A similar pattern developed in Canada and Britain, although British money and capital markets seemed to adjust more rapidly as inflation rates soared over 20 percent in certain years. The combination of low real rates of return, staggering oil bills and declining industrial productivity, aggravated by myopic government regulation, led to a deteriorating U.S. balance of payments. Foreign exchange markets took the weaker currencies to lower and more uncertain levels. From 1971 to the end of 1980, spot DM ascended as follows:

DM to One...	1971	End of 1980	Percent Appreciation
U.S. dollar	3.20	1.72	86
Can. dollar	2.90	1.30	123
Pound sterling	8.32	3.83	117

During the same period, the exchange markets became deeper and better able to provide forward hedging and covering.

The volatility of spot and forward exchange rates was often more important to private transactors than trends in exchange-rate levels. Swings of 20 to 30 percent in a year or two were common. The U.S. dollar rebounded after 1973, declined in 1975, recovered again until 1977, and then began a protracted decline with a brief respite from November 1978 to June 1979. In late 1980, the dollar again reversed field, displaying considerable strength, and continued to grow throughout the first half of 1981.

Month-to-month variations in 10 exchange rates from 1972, the first year of flexible rates, through 1980 are plotted in Charts 1 through 4. This record, when presented in Appendix 3 in terms of annualized monthly percentage variations, shows over 6 percent of the observations during 1978–80 exceeding a 100 percent annual change. Note the especially sharp shifts between successive months in 1978 in the strength of the dollar and pound relative to each other and to other major currencies.

	Annualized Percent Appreciation (+) or Depreciation (−)	
	Mid-Aug. to Mid-Sept. 1978	Mid-Sept. to Mid-Oct. 1978
U.S.$ against pound	− 44%	+ 109%
U.S.$ against DM	− 70	+ 199
U.S.$ against Swiss franc	− 34	+ 434
U.S.$ against yen	− 48	+ 211
Pound against DM	− 46	+ 43
Pound against Swiss franc	+ 18	+ 156
Pound against yen	− 6	+ 49

Tables 1 through 4 summarize the annualized percentage appreciation and depreciation over the same nine-year period of the 10 pairs of currencies in terms of their arithmetic means and standard deviations. Daily variations of 4 or 5 percent are common. Increased exchange-rate volatility is also reflected in wider bid-offer spreads indicating the increased cost of transacting.

Of course, many of these variations cancel over time, but this may be little comfort to the financial manager with limited time horizons and complex financial commitments. Moreover, the counsel of efficient-markets advocates must be examined in light of the forecasting experience implicit in forward markets. Cases have been documented of systematic underprediction when the spot exchange rate is rising and overprediction when it is declining.[1]

Central banks have intervened in exchange markets throughout the period of floating exchange rates, increasing the risk of speculators. Recent experience is reminiscent of the 1920s when the demise of the gold standard led to a floating exchange-rate system. However, this earlier period was characterized by a far more centralized international financial system, far fewer multinational corporations (MNCs) and other participants in international exchange markets, and less extensive use of discretionary monetary policy for domestic stabilization.

The monetary laxity displayed by governments in the 1970s contrasts sharply with the 1920s. The collapse of the gold standard, forced upon governments by war financing needs, was accepted without great enthusiasm. Indeed, despite Keynes' admonitions, the return to gold parity was actively sought by Great Britain, the United States and France as unemployment increased. Freedom from the gold standard's discipline was considered neither desirable nor even feasible. As 1981 began, gold was in the range of U.S. $500 to $600 per ounce, after having soared to over $800, and except for a handful of the more extreme "supplysiders," few now advocate a return to the gold standard.[2]

The Role of the MNC

In the 1920s, corporate cash flows were rarely denominated in a variety of currencies. Some companies, mostly primary materials producers, did have production facilities abroad, but this geographical dispersion was largely an accident of geology. Moreover, royalty payments were almost invariably denominated in sterling or U.S. dollars rather than in the local currency. Exchange risk was borne primarily by local participants, and cross-border corporate cash flows were limited. Individuals, banks

---

1 See J.M. Blin, "Forward Rates as Predictors of Future Spot Rates: An Econometric Analysis," *Empirical Economics*, forthcoming.

2 Note, however, that the monetary uses of gold—as a domestic monetary base or in international settlements—are still being very much debated, as evidenced by President Reagan's recent creation of a commission to examine the monetary role of gold.

CHART 1: **MONTHLY EXCHANGE-RATE MOVEMENTS, 1972–80**
(Pound and Deutsche Mark per Dollar)

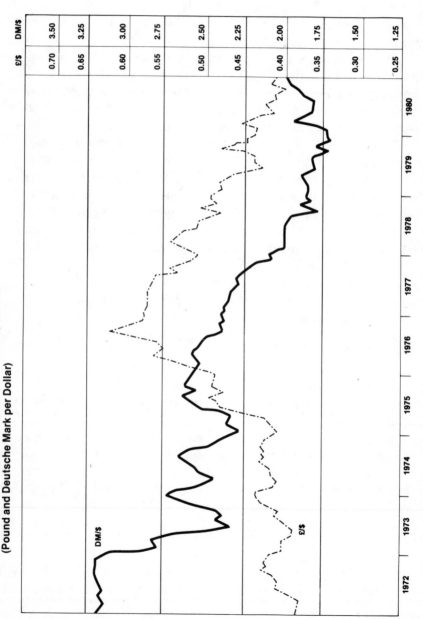

Source: Data (percentage annualized) are provided by the National Westminster Bank Ltd.

TABLE 1: AVERAGE ANNUALIZED MONTHLY PERCENTAGE CHANGES OF MAJOR EXCHANGE RATES, 1972-80[1]
(U.S.$ against Pound and Deutsche Mark)

	1972	1973	1974	1975	1976	1977	1978	1979	1980
U.S.$ against pound									
Mean	13.2%	8.6%	-2.6%	21.0%	28.6%	-9.8%	6.1%	-3.1%	0.3%
Standard deviation	38.6	29.6	20.2	31.7	54.2	19.1	46.1	42.3	32.8
Adjusted for Euro-currency interest rates[2]									
Mean	10.3	4.9	-8.3	16.1	20.2	-12.8	4.0	-6.8	-3.6
Standard deviation	39.5	29.5	23.4	31.9	55.8	18.2	47.0	42.3	33.3
Adjusted for domestic interest rates[2]									
Mean	10.9	5.6	-5.3	16.4	21.9	-12.3	4.8	-7.0	-4.2
Standard deviation	39.0	29.9	21.6	31.9	55.9	18.3	46.4	42.4	33.3
U.S.$ against DM									
Mean	-1.4	5.8	-10.0	19.6	-5.4	-10.6	4.4	-3.4	33.9
Standard deviation	7.7	63.4	33.8	56.8	18.9	17.1	70.1	26.6	64.9
Adjusted for Euro-currency interest rates									
Mean	0.7	8.9	-8.9	21.1	-4.3	-9.1	9.1	1.5	41.2
Standard deviation	8.7	61.9	35.6	56.8	19.1	17.0	70.4	26.6	66.3
Adjusted for domestic interest rates									
Mean	-2.2	2.9	-9.3	20.8	-4.5	-9.4	8.7	1.1	37.0
Standard deviation	8.5	63.1	35.1	56.9	18.8	16.8	70.4	26.4	66.2

[1]All figures in Tables 1–4 are computed from annualized monthly exchange-rate data supplied by the National Westminster Bank. See Appendix 3 for data from which the first pairs of figures at current month's exchange rates are computed.

[2]These two sets of figures, computed on the bases of current month's exchange rates plus Euro-currency interest rates and at current month's exchange rates plus domestic interest rates, are to be read in view of (a) the existence of interest-rate arbitrage between currencies, whereby the forward premium (or discount) on a currency is nearly equal to the interest-rate differential between instruments of similar risk and maturity denominated in the two currencies, and (b) the fact that forward rates—priced on whatever basis (in particular, the interest differential basis as noted in [a])—are seldom an accurate predictor of the subsequent spot rates or changes thereof.

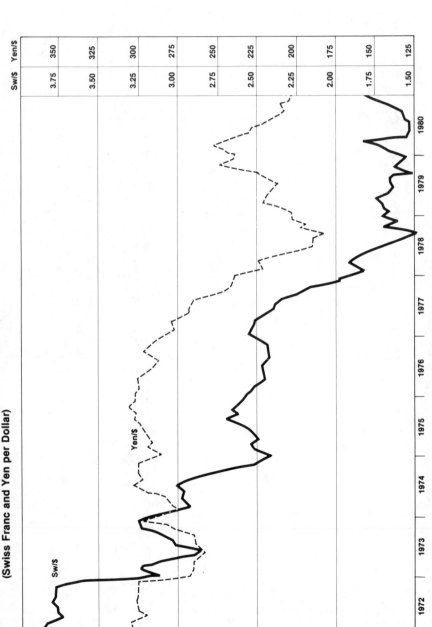

CHART 2: **MONTHLY EXCHANGE-RATE MOVEMENTS, 1972–80**
(Swiss Franc and Yen per Dollar)

Source: Data (percentage annualized) are provided by the National Westminster Bank Ltd.

TABLE 2: AVERAGE ANNUALIZED MONTHLY PERCENTAGE CHANGES OF MAJOR EXCHANGE RATES, 1972-80[1]
(U.S.$ against Swiss Franc and Yen)

	1972	1973	1974	1975	1976	1977	1978	1979	1980
U.S.$ against Swiss franc									
Mean	-5.3%	5.6%	-19.4%	14.2%	-2.5%	-17.8%	22.2%	3.3%	40.2%
Standard deviation	15.1	55.1	26.7	55.6	15.5	22.6	139.8	44.1	59.7
Adjusted for Euro-currency interest rates									
Mean	-2.4	9.3	-18.7	17.5	1.3	-14.7	29.7	12.6	39.4
Standard deviation	16.2	55.7	27.6	55.7	15.4	22.3	140.4	44.2	62.5
Adjusted for domestic interest rates									
Mean	-2.8	10.0	-15.1	16.6	1.3	-14.5	29.4	12.8	38.9
Standard deviation	15.4	55.9	27.4	55.5	15.5	22.3	140.3	44.0	61.9
U.S.$ against yen									
Mean	-2.0	10.6	3.9	3.4	-4.1	-14.5	2.0	25.0	-5.0
Standard deviation	14.1	48.4	31.1	16.7	15.1	17.2	75.8	41.3	42.3
Adjusted for Euro-currency interest rates									
Mean	-1.7	12.6	1.8	-1.2	-6.0	-13.1	8.7	30.3	-3.3
Standard deviation	14.4	47.9	32.1	16.5	15.2	17.2	77.1	41.4	43.4
Adjusted for domestic interest rates									
Mean	-2.3	11.8	1.6	-1.4	-6.1	-14.7	5.4	30.0	-3.5
Standard deviation	14.4	47.9	31.8	16.8	15.1	17.0	76.4	41.5	41.7

[1]See footnotes to Table 1.

CHART 3:   MONTHLY EXCHANGE-RATE MOVEMENTS, 1972–80
(Deutsche Mark, Yen and Swiss Franc per Pound)

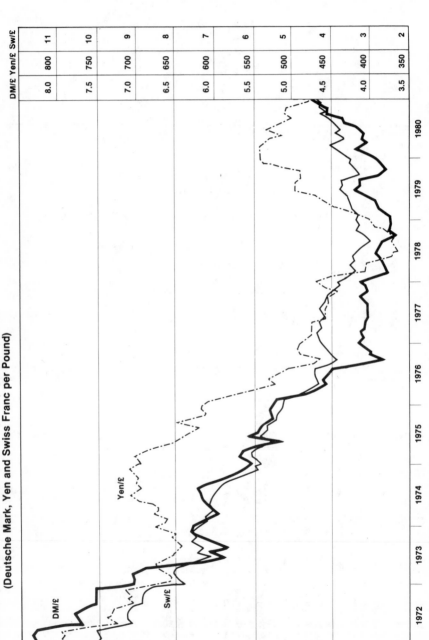

Source: Data (percentage annualized) are provided by the National Westminster Bank Ltd.

TABLE 3: AVERAGE ANNUALIZED MONTHLY PERCENTAGE CHANGES OF MAJOR EXCHANGE RATES, 1972–80[1]
(Pound against Deutsche Mark, Swiss Franc and Yen)

	1972	1973	1974	1975	1976	1977	1978	1979	1980
Pound against DM									
Mean	-7.0%	-6.5%	-6.3%	0.4%	-12.2%	1.2%	-4.9%	11.6%	40.2%
Standard deviation	19.7	41.4	20.7	43.7	41.2	19.0	29.4	34.3	55.0%
Adjusted for Euro-currency interest rates									
Mean	-2.0	30.1	-2.5	6.9	-2.7	5.7	1.9	19.4	48.3
Standard deviation	21.7	41.2	19.5	43.2	43.1	18.9	29.8	34.6	55.7
Adjusted for domestic interest rates									
Mean	-5.5	-6.4	-5.9	6.2	-4.6	4.9	0.7	19.2	47.7
Standard deviation	20.1	41.6	19.7	43.6	43.0	18.8	30.1	34.5	55.5
Pound against Swiss franc									
Mean	-10.3	-4.7	-17.2	-4.3	-7.3	-8.5	0.2	16.1	30.2
Standard deviation	22.8	42.6	19.9	43.8	47.4	18.7	59.6	37.2	42.3
Adjusted for Euro-currency interest rates									
Mean	-4.6	2.6	-10.9	3.9	4.9	-2.4	9.8	28.2	42.0
Standard deviation	24.3	43.0	19.8	43.7	49.5	20.2	60.2	37.3	42.4
Adjusted for domestic interest rates									
Mean	-5.6	2.6	-10.3	2.7	3.2	-2.7	8.7	28.7	42.1
Standard deviation	23.2	42.9	20.2	43.7	49.5	20.5	60.2	37.1	42.1
Pound against yen									
Mean	-6.2	0.5	7.4	-11.7	-13.3	-1.9	-5.2	47.8	-3.2
Standard deviation	25.5	33.6	27.9	17.1	37.6	25.5	38.1	73.6	36.6
Adjusted for Euro-currency interest rates									
Mean	-3.1	6.1	11.0	-11.4	-6.8	2.5	3.7	55.9	20.2
Standard deviation	27.6	34.0	27.0	17.8	40.1	26.1	40.2	73.5	43.2
Adjusted for domestic interest rates									
Mean	3.8	4.6	7.7	-11.9	-8.6	0.4	-0.4	55.9	2.3
Standard deviation	39.8	33.8	27.8	18.0	39.7	25.3	39.5	73.5	39.0

[1] See footnotes to Table 1.

CHART 4:   MONTHLY EXCHANGE-RATE MOVEMENTS, 1972–80
(Swiss Franc and Yen per Deutsche Mark and Yen per Swiss Franc)

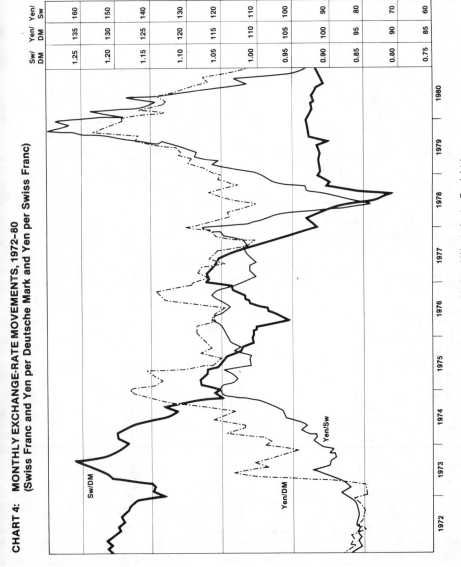

Source: Data (percentage annualized) are provided by the National Westminster Bank Ltd.

TABLE 4: AVERAGE ANNUALIZED MONTHLY PERCENTAGE CHANGES OF MAJOR EXCHANGE RATES, 1972-80[1]
(Deutsche Mark against Swiss Franc and Yen; Swiss Franc against Yen)

	1972	1973	1974	1975	1976	1977	1978	1979	1980
DM against Swiss franc									
Mean	-3.7%	7.3%	-7.8%	-5.1%	5.8%	-8.7%	6.0%	3.8%	-2.1%
Standard deviation	10.8	33.6	18.6	12.4	19.7	17.3	50.7	15.3	14.7
Adjusted for Euro-currency interest rates									
Mean	-3.6	7.9	-8.3	-3.4	8.5	-7.1	8.9	8.1	1.6
Standard deviation	11.6	33.6	18.1	13.0	20.1	17.6	50.9	15.5	14.7
Adjusted for domestic interest rates									
Mean	-1.1	14.6	-4.3	-3.9	8.6	-6.6	9.0	8.8	1.9
Standard deviation	10.4	34.0	19.0	12.4	20.0	17.7	50.8	15.6	14.6
DM against yen									
Mean	-0.7	27.9	22.8	-4.1	5.1	-1.7	5.7	38.1	-7.9
Standard deviation	11.4	72.4	36.1	25.4	27.2	25.7	47.3	61.0	48.7
Adjusted for Euro-currency interest rates									
Mean	-2.6	26.8	19.5	-10.3	2.1	-1.8	7.8	38.5	-10.3
Standard deviation	11.4	72.4	36.5	25.5	27.2	26.7	47.7	60.9	49.2
Adjusted for domestic interest rates									
Mean	-0.3	32.0	19.7	-10.1	2.2	-3.1	4.9	38.6	1.2
Standard deviation	12.1	73.1	36.1	25.6	27.1	25.9	47.4	61.0	50.1
Swiss franc against yen									
Mean	5.4	19.6	38.5	2.8	1.1	11.3	14.5	37.2	-56.4
Standard deviation	20.1	49.1	52.7	32.3	24.2	39.3	66.8	68.1	71.1
Adjusted for Euro-currency interest rates									
Mean	2.8	17.9	35.8	-5.1	-4.6	9.5	13.8	33.2	-32.5
Standard deviation	21.7	50.3	52.3	33.0	24.2	40.9	67.2	67.7	63.2
Adjusted for domestic interest rates									
Mean	2.6	16.4	32.0	-4.4	-4.7	7.7	10.8	32.7	21.8
Standard deviation	20.8	48.9	52.7	32.6	24.1	39.8	66.9	67.8	70.7

[1]See footnotes to Table 1.

and nonfinancial corporations engaged in international portfolio diversification, but governments kept their official reserves largely in gold and sterling. In contrast, contemporary MNCs, with research, production and marketing facilities dispersed worldwide, have assets, liabilities and cash flows denominated in a wide variety of currencies. Consequently, managerial decisions regarding trade, investment and finance must be made in view of both financial and nonfinancial market conditions.

The Regulatory Framework

The regulatory framework encompasses three areas—foreign exchange and taxation, banking and financial reporting.

Foreign Exchange and Taxation

The strict foreign exchange controls to which U.K. residents were subject throughout the post-World War II period were finally dismantled in autumn 1979. Previously, access to foreign exchange markets had been restricted to stem capital outflows and reduce pressure against sterling. Foreign investment by U.K. residents was discouraged by requiring the purchase of foreign exchange on a two-tier market where net sellers were required to convert into sterling. Excess demand for foreign exchange for investment resulted in a substantial premium on U.S. dollars. The Bank of England monitored the exchange controls and also limited access to forward markets.

These regulations encouraged U.K. companies to manage their exchange risk in innovative ways. Foreign growth strategies, financing and corporate plans were palpably complicated by the exchange controls, but this experience trained British firms to deal with the heightened exchange risk of the 1970s. Regulation creates a market for risk-shifting ingenuity. In contrast, American firms had far less experience in dealing with currency problems. This distinction between British and U.S. firms is noted later in our empirical work.

Although exchange controls were shunned for the most part in the United States, from 1964 to 1974 direct capital outflows were restricted to reduce the U.S. balance-of-payments deficit. Chief among the measures were the 1963 Interest Equalization Tax (IET), controls administered by the Office of Foreign Direct Investment, and the voluntary credit restraint program. The IET sought to equalize the cost for foreign corporations raising debt capital in the United States. Before IET, the greater depth of U.S. capital markets made U.S. financing preferable for many foreign borrowers. The main beneficiaries of these measures were the City of London and the Euro-bond market. Debt issues, underwritten by major international investment banking houses, became another addition to the already thriving international financial role of London. From an annual volume of approximately $1 billion in the mid 1960s, new Euro-bond issues grew to over $20 billion annually by the end of the '70s, providing an alternative financing source to U.S.-based firms. The capital control measures encouraged the use of local capital markets as well as the local accumulation of foreign earnings.

The size of a forward foreign exchange contract needed to cover a given balance sheet exposure is affected by the prevailing tax rate. (See Chapter II for a discussion of balance sheet exposure.) If forward contracts are used for covering balance sheet exposure, not a widespread practice, then the amount of forward cover demanded would be magnified as a result of tax considerations.[3]

Banking

Banking regulations have been as important as foreign exchange and tax regulations, especially in the United States. Most notable among these were the reserve requirements imposed on Federal Reserve member banks' various liabilities and deposit interest-rate ceilings. These restrictions expelled the offshore money market from the United States and helped establish the City of London as the leading international financial center.[4]

---

3 A discussion of tax effects can be found in D.F. Landry, "Tax and Accounting Effects of Foreign Currency Fluctuations," *The Tax Executive* (January 1976), pp. 125-47; and P.B. Musgrave, "Exchange Rate Aspects in the Taxation of Foreign Income," *National Tax Journal* (December 1975), pp. 405-513.

4 For example, see G. Kanatas and S.I. Greenbaum, "Bank Reserve Requirements and Monetary Aggregates," Banking Research Center Working Paper #55, April 1981, North-western University. The role of these regulations in the growth of the Euro-dollar market is discussed by R.I. McKinnon, *Money in International Exchange: The Convertible Currency System* (Oxford University Press, 1979), especially Chapter 9; and J. Niehans and J. Hewson, and "The Eurodollar Market and Monetary Theory," *Journal of Money, Credit and Banking,* 1976.

Financial Reporting

Financial reporting requirements are allegedly influential in the management of foreign exchange risk. The disparate requirements in Canada, Britain and the United States presumably have shaped attitudes toward management of foreign exchange exposure.

The *Canadian Institute of Chartered Accountants* (CICA) recommends that "at the transaction date, each asset, liability, revenue or expense arising from a foreign currency transaction of a domestic enterprise should be translated into Canadian dollars by the use of the exchange rate in effect at that date, except where there is a forward exchange contract which hedges a specifically identified transaction."[5] In brief, *current* exchange rates are the basis for translation. As for exchange gains and losses, a distinction must be drawn between three situations: (a) those that both arise and are realized during the current period, (b) those that arise but remain unrealized during the current period, and (c) other unrealized gains and losses. Realized exchange-rate gains and losses are to be included in net income for that period. Unrealized gains and losses arising in the current period are also to be included in net income while others are to be amortized over the remaining life of the asset or liability.

The *Accounting Standards Committee* (ASC) in Britain published exposure draft 21 which concludes that *both* current exchange rates (the closing method) and historic exchange rates (the temporal method) can be used. Reserve accounts, "offsetting" between long-term liabilities and the fixed assets they financed, and amortization all are allowed in reporting realized and unrealized gains and losses subject to certain guidelines.[6]

The *Federal Accounting Standards Board* (FASB) in the United States produced Statement No. 8 in October 1975, which applies to all U.S. reporting corporations as of January 1976. Monetary items including long-term liabilities are translated at current exchange rates, whereas nonmonetary items (fixed assets and inventory) are translated at historic exchange rates. Both realized and

---

5 CICA, "Accounting Recommendations" (September 1978), General Accounting Section 1650.

6 ASC, "Accounting for Foreign Currency Transactions" (September 1977).

unrealized gains and losses are to be reflected in current income. Reserve accounts and deferrals are prohibited.

FASB No. 8 has been a source of heated controversy since its inception. The rule has effectively sensitized the reported earnings of U.S. MNCs to the oscillations of exchange rates, creating an unmistakable impression of heightened risk. For example, on April 9, 1980, ITT announced that the soaring value of the U.S. dollar in the first quarter of 1980 added about $1 a share to its quarterly earnings of $2.40 a share. A 64 percent increase in earnings over a year earlier would have been reduced to 4 percent without the foreign exchange gain. The impact of such earnings swings on share valuation has been the subject of several studies and remains controversial.[7] Suffice it to say that volatility of reported earnings may adversely affect market valuation of a company's shares. In August 1980, responding to sharp criticism, the FASB proposed the following revisions to Statement No. 8.[8]

(1) Most balance sheet translation gains and losses would not pass through income, but would be reflected directly as an adjustment to stockholders' equity. However, exchange gains and losses arising from individual foreign transactions would still be included in income.

(2) Current exchange rates would be used for converting *all* assets and liabilities rather than only monetary assets.

(3) In some cases, a currency other than the local currency may be used for carrying local assets and liabilities.

If adopted, these revisions would move the U.S. standards closer to the Canadian and British guidelines.[9]

Summary

This brief review of regulations affecting corporate handling of foreign exchange risk suggests two points. (1) Diversity of tax,

---

7 For example, see J.K. Shank, J.F. Dillard and R.J. Murdock, *Assessing the Economic Impact of FASB No. 8* (Financial Executives Research Foundation, 1979).

8 For a discussion of the proposed changes, see *Foreign Currency Translation, An Overview of the New FASB Exposure Draft* (New York: Peat, Marwick, Mitchell and Co., September 1980).

9 On June 30, 1981, following a review of comments to the exposure draft, the FASB came out with a slightly altered version of the 1980 revision, designed to avoid some possible misuses of the standard.

banking, foreign exchange market, and reporting regulations has been the rule; and (2) regulations have produced innovative solutions to financing and exposure problems.

THE PROBLEM OF FOREIGN EXCHANGE RISK

Flexible exchange rates have exacerbated the problem of exchange risk management for corporations dealing in several currencies. For many, exchange risk is a compelling daily concern requiring substantial resource commitments. The following is a simplified description of the problem.

Problem Statement

Consider a U.S. corporation with one foreign subsidiary, whose balance sheet, denominated in local currency (LC), is shown in Table 5. For accounting purposes, a U.S.$/LC exchange rate must be selected in order to translate. Should the exchange rate be that prevailing at the date of translation (the current rate), when the asset (or liability) was acquired (the historic rate), or at another date? The choice is usually one or some combination of the following three alternatives.

Current or Closing Exchange-Rate Method

The use of current exchange rates to translate all items—long- and short-term, monetary and nonmonetary—is favored by many for its simplicity, consistency and intuitive appeal. The parent

TABLE 5:   BALANCE SHEET, SUBSIDIARY X LTD.
            (December 31, 1979)

Assets	LC	Current $ Value LC 2.0 = $1.00	Liabilities and Equity	LC	Current $ Value LC 2.0 = $1.00
Current			Liabilities		
Cash & accts. rec.	5.6	2.8	Short-term debt	5.0	2.5
Inventories	4.4	2.2	Long-term debt	9.0	4.5
Net plant	10.0	5.0	Equity	6.0	3.0
Total	20.0	10.0	Total	20.0	10.0

company's equity in the subsidiary results in a long local currency position. Hence, a depreciation of the parent's currency will yield foreign exchange gains while an appreciation will yield losses. This approach views the parent's exposure as being limited to the equity position in the subsidiary. In an inflationary domestic context, replacement cost accounting is based on similar considerations. The current exchange-rate translation is often criticized because fixed assets frequently are naturally hedged since an appreciation of the local currency leads to a bidding up of the local currency price of plant and equipment and similar assets. Thus, if long-term currency debt becomes more costly to repay in terms of the parent's currency, the loss is offset by a higher market value of fixed assets.

Current/Noncurrent or Working Capital Method

According to the working capital method, items scheduled to be received or paid within one year are translated at current exchange rates whereas longer-term items are translated at historic exchange rates. Since the local currency price of long-term assets often varies with that currency's value, a revaluation should lead to a bidding up of the domestic price of long-term assets. This might be expected if the long-term assets produced services not exposed to import competition. Then, these assets would be naturally hedged against exchange-rate variation, and translation at current exchange rates would be inappropriate unless the assets were simultaneously inflated in the domestic currency.

Monetary/Nonmonetary or Historic Method

The historic exchange-rate method of translation distinguishes financial and physical items. Physical assets are translated at historic exchange rates whether short-term (inventory) or long-term (plant), while financial assets and liabilities are translated at current exchange rates, irrespective of term to maturity. This approach introduces an asymmetry between translated fixed assets and their financing counterparts. The experience of U.S. corporations with long-term Swiss franc liabilities booked in the early 1970s illustrates the difficulties of reporting under these rules.

These three basic translation methods, or variants of the three, have been used at various times in different countries. The con-

TABLE 6:   MEASURING TRANSLATION EXPOSURE FOR SUBSIDIARY X LTD.
(Exchange Rate: LC 2.0 = $1.10)*

Method	Exposed Assets	Exposed Liabilities	Net Exposure	Accounting Gain (Loss)
Current rate	$10,000	$7,000	$3,000	$300
Current/noncurrent	5,000	2,500	2,500	250
Monetary/nonmonetary	2,800	7,000	(4,200)	(420)

*As of December 31, 1980, compared to LC 2.0 = $1.00 on December 31, 1979.

trast between net exposure under these alternatives is illustrated in Table 6, where we assume that Subsidiary X had been incorporated on December 31, 1979, when LC 2.0 equalled U.S. $1.00, and the local currency appreciated 10 percent in the subsequent year.

Thus far, our discussion has focused on the measurement of foreign exchange gains and losses. A final point relates to how these are to be displayed. Some maintain that, in the spirit of full disclosure, such gains and losses should flow through income in the period they are recognized (not necessarily realized). Others favor the more traditional approach of amortizing gains and losses through the use of reserve accounts. This is tantamount to applying an arbitrary smoothing rule to earnings since such gains and losses presumably are uncontrollable and tend to offset each other through time. In something of a compromise, the proposed revision of FASB No. 8 would recognize translation gains and losses contemporaneously, but they would be recorded directly in an equity subaccount and not flow through net income. This approach insulates the income statement from the vagaries of translations but retains balance sheet sensitivity; the income statement is smoothed infinitely and the balance sheet not at all.

Transaction Versus Translation Exposure

A distinction is commonly made between exchange gains and losses arising from known forthcoming exchanges across currencies and those arising from the periodic restatement of foreign subsidiary accounts in terms of the parent company's currency. The former *transaction exposure* can be illustrated by an order being placed today for a foreign purchase requiring payment at a known time in the future. The latter *translation exposure* is reflected in the parent's periodic need to report a balance sheet to its stockholders and other constituents. Transaction exposure is contractual, is readily accessible to measurement and normally has immediate cash flow and tax implications. In contrast, translation exposure may have neither immediate tax nor cash flow implications. The exposure arises from the need to record the ownership of foreign assets or liabilities in the parent's financial statements.

If forward cover is purchased in the market, the overall cash impact of transaction exposure is the sum of the cash impact of the exposed transaction *plus* that of the forward hedge. The cash impact of a covered translation exposure is limited to that arising from the forward contract. If aftertax zero translation loss is sought, the cash impact is magnified by the corporate income tax. For example, if the tax rate is 50 percent, the forward contract should be twice that of the initial exposure.

Hedging translation exposure gives rise to cash flows that are unrelated to immediate reciprocal trade flows. In terms of balance of payments, forward market cover of translation exposure would increase autonomous short-term capital flows. Increases in domestic holdings of foreign assets or liabilities or the corporate tax rate, or perhaps the level of net book exposure resulting from a new accounting convention, would lead to increased and recurring short-term capital flows.

Economic Exposure

Like accounting exposure, the concept and consequently the measurement of economic exposure is not well defined.[10] The economic concept of exposure seeks to measure the degree to which future cash flows are affected by exchange-rate volatility. Economists emphasize economic or market values and hence are concerned with the impact of exchange rates on future financial statements when entries are evaluated at current market rather

---

10 See J.M. Burns, *Accounting Standards and International Finance: With Special Reference to Multinationals* (American Enterprise Institute, September 1976); and R.A. Aliber, *Exchange Risk and Corporate International Finance* (Macmillan Press, 1978).

than book value. They stress a functional link between exchange rates and the objects of adjustment, the cash flow or its present value. Thus, an autonomous exchange-rate variation not only affects the domestic currency value of commitments, but also alters expected sales (purchases), revenues (costs) and profits (losses) associated with the foreign commitment. Accounting approaches tend to adjust commitments for exchange-rate variations while viewing the objects of adjustment as mostly predetermined.

This difference is highlighted in the distinction between contractual and noncontractual cash flows. The former usually have a known maturity and magnitude even if they are denominated in a foreign currency. Forward markets can be used to lock in the value of contractual flows. But exposures arising from noncontractual cash flows are less well defined and, consequently, are less amenable to straightforward hedging transactions. Exchange-rate fluctuations affect market potential—domestic and foreign—according to supply and demand elasticities. The corporations' uncertain noncontractual flows are difficult to hedge via forward or money markets because their magnitudes and timing are unknown.

The equity shares of MNCs reflect noncontractual exchange risk; each share is a claim to a collection of uncertain returns denominated in many currencies. Not only are the returns in each country (currency) uncertain, as in any domestic corporation, but the aggregate of claims is also uncertain because of variable conversion ratios. Economic exposure emphasizes that the two sources of uncertainty are not independent. As exchange rates vary, they affect the sales and costs of each affiliate. For example, if a foreign subsidiary imports its raw materials, which account for 25 percent of total production costs, depreciation of the local currency will increase the subsidiary's costs and reduce its profit margin. If its market is primarily local, the effect on earnings and sales (in local currency) can be sizable. Thus, by recognizing a link between a corporation's cash flows and exchange rates, the concept of economic exposure dimensionally expands the problem of exchange-rate volatility, and the impact on the value of MNC equity or debt capital is further complicated.

II. A Survey of International Business Behavior

Floating exchange rates have forced MNCs to manage exchange risk on a day-to-day basis for more than eight years. The evidence is available in a wide array of publications. However, most of the work focuses on macro public policy issues, problems of market participants or the efficiency of financial markets. This last type of study is illustrated by the "Group of Thirty's" recent monograph on floating rates and foreign exchange markets.[1] The study sought to ". . . ascertain the *views of market participants* in the principal market centers on the functioning of the foreign exchange markets since the advent of floating exchange rates. . . . The emphasis . . . was on collecting the raw data of market impressions on the functioning of the market."[2]

In contrast, this study describes how a three-country sample of companies approached the putative problems of exchange risk management in the recent floating exchange-rate environment. More specifically, we examine:

(1) How do firms measure exchange risk and adapt their reporting systems?

(2) What monitoring techniques and controls are used in managing exposure?

(3) Which instruments, internal or external, have been most widely employed to limit exposure?

(4) What impact have corporate adjustments to floating rates had on key economic variables such as trade and capital flows?

We focus on the practice of foreign exchange exposure management and the links between corporate behavior and the macro issues associated with flexible exchange rates. Our data are the actual experiences of a sample of major firms in the United States, the United Kingdom and Canada.

APPROACH

The study was developed in three stages: an initial problem review; interviews with a cross-section of U.S. and U.K. firms;

---

1 Exchange Markets Participants' Study Group, *The Foreign Exchange Markets under Floating Rates: A Study in International Finance* (New York, 1980).

2 Ibid., pp. 1–2.

TABLE 7:   COMPANIES AND OTHER ORGANIZATIONS INTERVIEWED

United Kingdom		United States
Companies	**Government Institutions**	**Companies**
Bowater*	Bank of England	American Express Int'l.
FOREX	U.K. Export Credit	Banking Corp.
British Petroleum*	Guarantee Dept.	Chase Manhattan Bank*
General Electric Co.	(ECGD)	Exxon*
Lloyd Bank Int'l.*	U.K. Dept. of Trade	FMC Corporation
Midland Bank*		General Electric*
Rio Tinto Zinc*		Ingersoll-Rand*
Selection Trust*		Northern Trust Co.*
Shell*		Occidental Petroleum*
Wilkinson Match		

*Indicates that the institution is represented on the BNAC.

and a questionnaire survey of a wider group of companies in the United States, Britain and Canada.

Interviews were conducted during 1979 in Chicago, London and New York with 21 institutions, ranging from manufacturing and mining to banking—including a central bank, a government export credit-assistance institution and a foreign exchange consulting firm (see Table 7). Coordination with the C.D. Howe Institute of Canada, the Canadian sponsor of the BNAC, allowed the findings to be related to Canadian experience, providing a third vantage point.

We designed a questionnaire, reproduced in Appendix 1, based on our interviews with the U.S. and U.K. firms. It was circulated in late 1979 to 41 U.S., U.K. and Canadian firms. Detailed responses of the 27 who completed the questionnaire are tabulated in Appendix 2. Among the respondents were 11 U.S., 13 U.K. and 3 Canadian firms. Exhibits 20-28 in Appendix 2 reveal the following profile of the 27 respondents.

Major industries (Exhibit 20). Three U.S. firms were banks and 3 were industrial equipment producers. The remaining respondents were electronics, information processing, chemical, and petroleum producers. Just over one-half the U.K. respondents were in banking, petroleum and mining and natural resources, with the remainder dispersed. Canadian respondents were a petroleum, a mining and a metal-working firm.

Total sales, 1978 (Exhibit 21). U.S. respondents' annual sales ranged from under $300 million to over $50 billion. Six of these 11 companies had annual sales in excess of $1 billion. U.K. respondents' annual sales ranged from under £200 million to over £10 billion; more than one-half had sales of less than £1 billion. Canadian firms ranged from C$1 billion to C$10 billion annually.

Foreign sales, 1978 (Exhibit 22). U.S. and Canadian firms had relatively less overseas sales than U.K. companies. Eight U.S. and 2 Canadian firms made under one-half of their total sales to foreign customers, while 7 U.K. firms exceeded this export performance. Their greater potential experience and exposure may help to explain why U.K. firms handled foreign exchange somewhat differently than their U.S. and Canadian counterparts.

Size and location of assets (Exhibits 23 and 24). U.S. firms were larger in terms of assets than their U.K. or Canadian counterparts. Two of the 3 Canadian firms held less than 10 percent of their assets abroad, while U.K. and U.S. firms held from 10 to 50 percent of assets overseas in, respectively, 5 out of 13 and 9 out of 11 cases.

Currency exposure (Exhibit 25). The currency exposures most frequently indicated by U.S. firms were sterling (8 firms); the deutsche mark, French franc and Italian lira (7 firms each); the Canadian dollar (6 firms); and the Australian dollar, Japanese yen and Swiss franc (5 firms each). Most common currency exposures for U.K. firms were the U.S. dollar (7 firms); deutsche mark (6 firms); Canadian dollar (5 firms); and French franc (4 firms). Canadian firms were exposed in U.S. dollars (3 firms) and sterling (2 firms), along with the Australian dollar, Japanese yen and Swedish krona (1 firm each). Among those listing currencies, U.S. firms averaged 8 currencies each, U.K. firms 4 each and Canadian companies less than 3 each.

International spread of production facilities (Exhibit 26). Two of the 3 Canadian firms produced in 1 or 2 countries whereas most U.S. and U.K. firms produced in over 10 countries. There appears to be little difference between U.S. and U.K. firms in terms of their spread of production facilities.

Finally, Exhibits 27 and 28 show the different distribution of *sales and revenues* in the three countries.

ISSUES ADDRESSED

The following issues were covered in the interviews and in the questionnaire.

(1) How is foreign exchange risk perceived and measured?
(2) How is it monitored?
(3) How is it controlled?
(4) Who within the firm has responsibility for exposure management?
(5) What impact have floating rates had on financial reporting?
(6) What impact have floating rates had on the organizational structure of the firm?
(7) What effect have floating rates had on pricing, invoicing, inventory management, direct investment, and financial structure?

FINDINGS

The findings discussed here are based both on the responses to the questionnaire and on the interviews conducted preliminary to its design and distribution.

Defining and Measuring Exchange Risk

As indicated earlier, interpretations of foreign exchange exposure vary considerably. Accounting regulations and practices differ widely, but, more basically, economic exposure is not a well-defined concept. To plumb the perception as well as the measurement of foreign exchange risk, the questionnaire addressed financial reporting practices and managerial accounting adjustments made in the light of perceived exchange exposure.

Reporting practices varied among countries but not within countries. U.S. firms, constrained by FASB No. 8, used current bases for valuing current assets and all liabilities and historic bases for other accounts. U.K. companies used the current-rate method for valuing all accounts, and Canadian firms used current bases for current assets, inventories and short-term liabilities (the current/noncurrent method). Only 1 U.K. firm deviated in its external reports (Exhibit 1-a). Each country's accounting standards and laws constrain the choice of accounting procedures. Nevertheless, 8 out of 14 respondents indicated accuracy of valuation or ease of use as their reasons for present reporting practices (Exhibit 1-b).

Eight out of 27 respondents indicated that some internal adjustments for economic exposure were undertaken (Exhibit 2-a). Almost 50 percent of U.S. firms, but only 15 percent of U.K. firms, undertook economic exposure adjustments, which varied widely from hedging to altering account balances on the basis of foreign subsidiaries' ability to adjust prices. Three U.S. firms adjusted inventories for economic exposure (Exhibit 2-b).

Objectives and Strategies of Foreign Exchange Risk Management

A number of possible objectives were proposed in Question 3, ranging from avoiding major foreign exchange losses to minimizing earnings fluctuations and reductions in exposure. Avoidance of major loss was the most frequently indicated objective, taking 40 percent of U.K. responses, 30 percent of U.S. and 25 percent of Canadian. The U.S. firms expressed concern with economic exposure more frequently than U.K. or Canadian companies and also tended to have more complex objectives in foreign exchange management. The British were more concerned with maximizing home currency equivalent income than the Americans, which may reflect their longer experience with currency devaluation. U.S. firms displayed disparate objectives, those of U.K. firms were more focused (Exhibit 3).

Organizational Responses

Exhibit 4 shows that responsibility for foreign risk management tended to be less centralized among U.K. firms, who typically delegated the responsibility or shared it with subsidiaries. Only one U.K. company totally centralized foreign exchange management responsibility, whereas six U.S. and two Canadian firms did.

Interviews indicated that the pattern of response to heightened exchange risk among North American corporations has been reasonably well defined. Typically, foreign currency-denominated contractual cash flows are reported to a central treasury function. Exchange exposure reports, both for transactions and translations, are submitted frequently and at regular intervals according to a detailed format showing items, amounts, currency of denomination, and dates of commitments. Any foreign currency-denominated commitment exceeding a stipulated amount is typically cleared with the central treasury group. The result is structured reporting and systematic central authorization for substantial commitments. Variations among North American companies are numerous, as managerial styles and philosophies differ. In some cases, non-negligible resources—manpower, material, information systems—have been diverted to managing foreign exchange exposure.

Exhibits 5-a, b and c provide further assessment of the impact of flexible rates on the corporate organization. No significant change in the staffing of the foreign exchange risk management function was indicated by four U.S. and four U.K. companies and one Canadian firm (Exhibit 5-a). More of the reported changes show U.S., U.K. and Canadian firms dealing with foreign exchange risk by increasing time spent on financial management and by increasing staff size and/or quality. In the United States, floating exchange rates also prompted more specialized use of subsidiary management and use of outside consultants. Some U.K. firms responded to exchange-rate volatility by adding a computer model (and support staff), a foreign exchange-rate committee and staff specialists.

Information systems (Exhibit 5-b) were adjusted comparably in all three countries. Of the 27 respondents, 17 indicated that some internal changes were necessitated by floating exchange rates, and 5 stated that the changes were part of the normal evolutionary process. Four reported that no changes were made. Some difference between countries existed in computerization, with 2 U.K. versus 1 U.S. firm adding computers and/or computer models.

Special foreign exchange committees were established by only 2 U.K. companies.

Responses to question 5-c indicated that the percentage change in costs was less for U.K. than for U.S. firms. Only five each of the U.K. and U.S. companies could give absolute or percentage cost changes. Among all respondents, nine indicated that few or no cost changes had occurred, five said that the change was not quantifiable or available, and one had no response.

In sum, there have been cases of organizational changes that have tended toward greater centralization and more sophisticated information and reporting systems that, in turn, have led to an increase in cost of uncertain magnitude.

Internal Exchange Risk Control

A number of nonmarket hedging techniques can be employed to shift risk. They include: currency of invoicing on inter- or intracompany transactions (Exhibits 6 and 7); pricing policies—frequency of change, fixed versus flexible prices, responsibility for pricing decisions (Exhibit 8); and invoicing policy—timing and terms of payment (Exhibit 9).

The most frequently mentioned techniques include the following.

(a) Prepayment of import commitments if denominated in a strong currency. Similarly, hard currency loan prepayments have been observed as exchange rates moved against the outstanding liability. Another approach adjusts the terms of payment between different units of a multinational. Leading and lagging adjustments are usually easier to effect at the centralized level after netting out interaffiliate exposure.

(b) In dealing with future positions, price adjustments may be used, which take the form of transfer pricing changes, local subsidiary price increases or export price increases. Alternatively, the currency of invoicing can sometimes be altered.

(c) A third method of internal hedging involves asset/liability management. This approach is discussed later.

(d) The export finance company is another vehicle for achieving internal hedging. An independent offshore company buys the export receivables of the group's affiliates. By centralizing these assets, the export finance subsidiary can more readily choose a mix of liabilities to match the dates, amounts and currencies. The export finance company may also ease the import exchange restrictions. Export subsidiaries also occasionally re-invoice and take title to the goods, thus affording greater legal recourse in case of customer default.

Questionnaire responses on these issues point to major differences in the treatment of intercompany transactions among countries (Exhibit 6). Six U.S firms invoiced in U.S. dollars whereas only two U.K. firms shipped exclusively in sterling. In the United States, two firms used parent and subsidiary's currency and one the exporting country's currency. In the United Kingdom, practice varied widely. In Canada, one firm used the parent company's currency, one a third country's and one had no foreign subsidiary.

For purposes of external invoicing, one-fourth of U.S. firms dealt exclusively in U.S. dollars, and over one-half invoiced in a combination of foreign and domestic currencies (Exhibit 7). No U.K. firm invoiced exclusively in sterling. The client's currency was used by 2 U.K. firms; the rest used a variety of currencies, as did Canadian firms. Note that trade in oil and most ores is usually denominated in U.S. dollars. Two out of the 3 Canadian respondents and 4 out of the 13 U.K. firms were in these industries. Throughout the questionnaire, market conditions were cited to explain why firms could not react to foreign exchange fluctuations by changing prices or invoicing methods. Primary materials are normally traded in competitive world markets where individual traders have little influence on either currency of denomination or price.

The increase in foreign exchange volatility increased the frequency of price changes, although more than one-half of all respondents stated that the change in frequency was either not significant or not applicable. All Canadian firms were affected as were about one-third each of U.S. and U.K. firms (Exhibit 8-a).

Over 90 percent of all firms indicated that the administrative costs associated with more frequent price adjustments either were not significant or not applicable. Only one U.S. and one U.K. company reported significant increases in administrative costs (Exhibit 8-b).

Fixed-price contracts also were not often affected. Slightly more than one-half of all firms indicated insignificant change in their willingness to quote fixed prices, and there were no significant differences between countries. Of those reporting some change, one U.S. firm increased the use of home-currency denominated contracts and one included an escalation clause. In this connection, Britain's Export Credit Guarantee Department (ECGD) offers an unusual cost-escalation coverage (including exchange-rate change) between tender of offer and acceptance. Two U.K. firms nevertheless used escalation and one used conversion clauses although market factors limit the ability of firms to alter contracts (Exhibit 8-c).

The locus of responsibility for pricing decisions does not seem to have been altered with the advent of floating exchange rates. About 80 percent of all respondents reported either no change or that the question was not applicable. Two U.K. and two U.S. firms shifted pricing responsibility to their headquarters whereas one U.S. company moved responsibility toward more local control (Exhibit 8-d).

Similarly, timing of invoicing was not greatly affected. Twenty-four out of 27 respondents reported no or very little effect or that the question was not applicable. In fact, all U.K. and Canadian companies were in these 3 categories along with 8 U.S. firms (Exhibit 9-a).

Terms of payments also were little affected. Twenty-three respondents replied not applicable or that no or very little effect on terms of payment had occurred. The 2 remaining U.K. firms tightened terms of payment or hedged by using forward contracts or money markets. The 2 remaining U.S. firms altered intercompany transactions or indicated that policy varied across countries (Exhibit 9-b).

As seen in Exhibits 6-9, although the currency of invoicing, for both internal and external transactions, and the frequency of price adjustments may have been affected somewhat, little if any change was reported in the availability of fixed-price contracts, on the locus of responsibility for pricing decisions, on the timing of invoicing, or on the terms of payment. Nevertheless, some differences between the U.S. and U.K. firms were noted. In particular, the latter seem more inclined to formalize policies on these issues.

Short-Term Market Hedging Strategies:
Forward and Money Markets

Frequency

Hedging strategies usually involve netting out of within-company transactions. The resulting open balance sheet positions give rise to translation exposure. Contractual cash flows into and out of the corporation give rise to transaction exposure. If forward exchange rates are unbiased predictors of future spot rates, it is allegedly counterproductive to hedge since the long-run cost of remaining unhedged (i.e., exposed) is likely to average out to zero whereas covering forward involves transaction costs. The problem, however, is that the long run is often far too long in light of reporting requirements and capital market imperfections. If all foreign exchange gains and losses must be reflected in current earnings, as is currently the case in the United States under FASB No. 8, an appeal to long-run tendencies is not persuasive. Earnings volatility becomes a quarterly or even monthly reality. Moreover, even if capital markets pierce the accounting veil and distinguish between durable and ephemeral exchange-related earnings variations, smoother earnings are usually preferred by lenders, stockholders and, perforce, management. However ill-informed, corporate treasurers often accept the known and visible cost of forward hedging in lieu of earnings volatility, despite admonitions to the contrary. This conclusion is supported by responses to the question on transaction exposure hedging (Exhibit 10). Nine of 11 U.S. firms hedged transaction exposure (the remaining 2 responded not applicable). Canadian and U.S. firms tended to hedge partially (3 firms always and 4 firms seldom for the American companies; 2 firms always and 1 seldom for the Canadians). U.K. firms hedged more frequently and more completely (5 firms partially, 3 firms completely). One U.K. firm hedged to an unstated degree if the forecasted and forward rates differed.

Translation hedges were undertaken less frequently (Exhibit 11). Nine U.K. companies, 1 U.S. and 1 Canadian avoided translation hedging. Four firms (2 U.S. and 2 U.K.) indicated they almost always hedged as completely as possible, while 4 firms (3 U.S. and 1 U.K.) almost always hedged partially. Two firms (1 U.K. and 1 Canadian) seldom hedged as completely as possible, and 5 firms (4 U.S. and 1 Canadian) hedged partially but seldom. One U.S. firm hedged to an unstated degree if the cost was in line with the possible loss.

Purpose of Hedging

In the United States, translation exposure is hedged to avoid adverse effects on reported earnings, as indicated by 10 of the 11 U.S. firms. The 6 U.K. firms that responded (1 noted not applicable) seemed to be more concerned with balance sheet exposure per se, expressing concern about matching liabilities and assets, balance sheet ratios and equity changes. Canadian firms hedged against borrowing and transactions exposure (Exhibit 12).

Short-Term Hedging Vehicles

Hedging strategies may involve forward sales (purchases) of foreign currency, in which case subsequent changes in the spot rate become immaterial, since the conversion value of these cash flows is ensured in the corporation's unit of account. Alternatively, one of the currencies may be borrowed with the proceeds invested in the other so that the receivable or payable is neutralized. To illustrate, if a Swiss franc receivable of SF 1 million is due in 90 days, we could borrow Swiss francs at, for instance, 3 percent per annum, convert to U.S. dollars and invest at 12 percent in the United States. Proceeds from the receivable would be used to repay the Swiss franc debt. As a result of covered interest arbitrage, the forward Swiss franc sale and the Swiss franc borrowing should produce equivalent results.

Despite theoretical equivalence, responses to question 13 indicated that forward markets are the preferred hedging vehicle.[3] Six of the 11 U.S. firms, 7 of the 13 U.K. firms, and all 3 Canadian firms relied primarily on forward markets for short-term hedging. Only 1 U.S. firm depended mostly on money markets, and 3 U.S. and 5 U.K. firms indicated use of both forward and money markets. One U.S. company used overseas financing (or other) companies in conjunction with the use of other markets (Exhibit 13).

---

3 Note, however, that the accounting treatment of the two methods differs. Forward contracts are off balance-sheet items whereas outright borrowing, conversion and investment in a currency are recorded.

Long-Term Hedging Strategies

Strategy Evaluation

Hedging offsets uncertain forward assets—denominated in another currency—with similar liabilities (in denomination and maturity) to insulate the net position in the base currency. While the hedging concept is clear in principle, application is often complicated. Perfect hedges are unavailable, especially for multinationals facing a wide variety of cash flows and maturities.

Forward markets become increasingly thin as delivery dates become more remote. Forward contracts—and Euro-currency deposits and loans—are usually readily available in all major currencies for up to 6 months hence. Approaching 12 months, however, the markets become much thinner. Beyond a year, transactions are often prohibitively expensive, measured either by the bid-ask spread or the interest-rate parity comparisons for similar instruments in the two currencies. These market limitations severely constrain the feasibility of external hedging and often necessitate alternative nonmarket techniques. These nonmarket hedging techniques developed in response to shortcomings of forward exchange and money markets and also in response to exchange controls.

Long-term hedging strategies are addressed in Exhibit 14. Interestingly, financing techniques seemed to be the dominant vehicle for achieving long-term hedging, with 8 of 27 respondents stating that they evaluated alternative local versus parent company currency-financing techniques. Adjusting the capitalization of overseas subsidiaries is never mentioned alone. In addition, more than one-half the respondents indicated a more complex approach to long-term hedging. This complexity was more apparent among U.S. than U.K. firms who favored matched financing.

Barter Financing Schemes

Back-to-back forwards or parallel loans were initiated over 12 years ago. They involve two separate loan agreements whereby, for example, a U.S. company lends dollars to a U.K. company, which lends a similar amount of sterling to the U.S. company. Each company charges prevailing domestic lending rates to the other. Each loan constitutes a debt on the company's balance sheet.

Long-term currency swaps are simpler than back-to-back loans since they involve one transaction rather than two. For example, a U.S. and a U.K. company would swap $10 million for £ 5 million for a period of up to 15 years, bypassing both the spot and forward markets. The only payment is the net interest differential between the two countries. For instance, if the U.K. long-term interest rate is 14 percent and the corresponding U.S. interest rate is 10 percent, the U.S. company would pay 4 percent annually to the U.K. company. Repayment is usually at the initial exchange rate since in theory any exchange-rate adjustment should be reflected in the interest-rate differential already paid over the life of the loan. Various clauses allowing for variable interest rates, catastrophic events (e.g., major currency realignments) and possible loan syndication are commonly included. The currency swap is usually treated as a balance sheet footnote item, therefore avoiding establishing translation exposure and also serving to circumvent exchange or capital controls. This may explain the large number of U.S./U.K. swaps in the past 10 years. Alternative forms of financing, including back-to-back loans, affect the debt-equity ratio and establish a net exposed position on the company's balance sheet. The currency swap arrangement provides flexible financing and exposure coverage while integrating the potential exchange-rate change through the payment of the net interest-rate differential. Allowing for a variable-rate differential, say, a spread over London Interbank Offered Rate (LIBOR) for each Euro-currency, provides the needed flexibility. The practice can be compared to "barter financing." Swaps are a young but growing financing vehicle among U.S., U.K., German, Dutch, and Canadian companies. In 1977, the worldwide volume of long-term currency swaps, spread over the above-mentioned currencies, was estimated to be $1 billion equivalent.

Choices Among Long-Term Hedging Schemes

The instrument most commonly used to effect long-term hedging was foreign currency-denominated debt instruments (Exhibit 15). Among all respondents, 85 percent used foreign debt alone or in combination with other strategies. Two U.S., five U.K. and two Canadian firms used foreign currency-denominated debt instruments exclusively. Only one (U.S.) firm used parallel, swap or back-to-back loans exclusively. No respondent used long-term forward contracts alone. When combining strategies, U.K. firms, with one exception, used swaps or back-to-back loans with foreign debt, and three U.K. companies used these two approaches along with long-term forward contracts. Four U.S. firms combined parallel, swap or back-to-back loans with long-term forward contracts, but none reported using all three approaches.

Decisionmaking Processes for Risk Management

Implementation of risk management strategies requires allocation of decisionmaking responsibility within the corporation. The major difference between U.S. and U.K. firms seems to be a somewhat greater decentralization of responsibility among the latter, at least at the implementation stage.

On average, however, in all three countries general policy regarding exchange exposure management was generally formulated by senior management at the headquarters level (Exhibit 16-a). Exhibits 16-b(1) and 16-b(2) indicate the dispersion of responsibility for data analysis and forecasting. These responsibilities also seemed to be concentrated at senior levels in the firm with limited evidence of decentralization.

The locus of responsibility for deciding which exposures to hedge is described in Exhibit 16-c. Here, again, responsibility was lodged at the senior management level, with subsidiaries and staff playing secondary roles. Development and implementation of hedging policies seemed to be less centralized (Exhibit 16-d). In one-fourth of all cases, subsidiaries had major responsibility, and in another six cases, subsidiaries managed jointly with headquarters.

Effects on Asset Management:
Inventories and Direct Foreign Investment

In addition to the financing techniques discussed above, asset management has been suggested as a method of controlling exchange risk. Currency denomination of inventories as well as inventory levels can be used for this purpose. In fact, however, changes in foreign currency-denominated inventories were negligible (Exhibit 17). Two-thirds of all firms reported no change, one-fourth said the question was not applicable, and the remainder indicated that the changes were not significant. Two U.S. and one Canadian firm, but no U.K. firm, acknowledged changes in inventory policy as a result of exchange exposure (Exhibit 18). However, most respondents reported no significant impact on inventory policy.

A final area of concern is direct foreign investment. If the cost of capital to multinational firms has been raised by floating rates, could the end result be a reduced incentive to foreign investment? This issue was addressed in a number of ways throughout our interviews. Although responses were mixed, with many indicating no effect of exchange-rate volatility on their direct investment, some replied that foreign investment hurdle rates had been elevated. More respondents emphasized greater reliance on more formal and exhaustive analyses. The direct investment issue also was addressed in our questionnaire (Exhibit 19).

Foreign asset acquisition seemed to have been affected somewhat among U.S. firms, but far less among those in the United Kingdom. For example, only 4 of the 11 U.S. firms versus 11 of the 16 U.K. and Canadian firms indicated either insignificant or no investment effects. Similarly, 4 of the 11 U.S. firms indicated more consideration of risk of fluctuating exchange rates, but only 2 of the 13 U.K. firms did so.

To summarize, the interviews and questionnaire responses illuminated many concerns about recent corporate experience with floating exchange rates. Flexible rates have sometimes fostered greater centralization of the group treasury function. Occasionally, they have affected the corporate structure, resource allocation and responsibilities for the financial and asset structure of the corporation. Some of these adjustments have affected day-to-day operations as well as long-run decisions. In the final chapter, we draw these diverse strands together and examine their impact. Our interpretations are compared with those of economists and central bankers. Of particular interest are the possible effects on capital and foreign exchange markets. Perhaps even more important are policy implications suggested by this analysis.

III. An Appraisal of Corporate Behavior and Public Policy Implications

The corporate experiences reported in Chapter II are at odds with suggestions often found in the international corporate finance literature.[1] For example, one appealingly simple and academically fashionable view urges complete passivity to exchange risk. At the other extreme, safety-first approaches dictate complete (in some sense) hedging programs. Not surprisingly, corporations occupy a middle ground in which exposure is carefully monitored and partial hedging is common. One interpretation of observed behavior is developed in this chapter. We are led to reflect on the meaning of corporate behavior as it adapts to the complex web of governmental regulations and market processes in an effort to control its risk exposure.

HEDGING: PRUDENT MANAGEMENT OR ILLUSORY INSURANCE?

The Case for Selective Hedging

The data and observations discussed in the previous chapter suggest that the volatility of exchange rates was manageable for firms, if at some cost. Selective hedging was widely observed in the survey, and this requires interpretation in light of the "efficient markets" argument.

First, investors presumably are capable of assessing the expected returns and risks of an investment portfolio and by judicious choice can select a preferred level of risk. Firms *qua* firms should be risk neutral, focusing exclusively on expected returns. Second, if foreign exchange markets are efficient in that spot and forward rates subsume all relevant information about currency values, and if forward rates are also unbiased estimators of future spot rates, hedging should prove counterproductive in the long run. Gains and losses will tend to offset each other, but

---

1 Summaries of these suggestions can be found in "International Trade and Investment under Flexible Exchange Rates," commentary by Dennis F. Logue in *Exchange Rate Flexibility*, J. Dreyer, G. Haberler and T.D. Willett, eds. (American Enterprise Institute, 1978). Also see R.A. Aliber, *Exchange Risk and Corporate International Finance* (The Macmillan Press Ltd., 1978).

hedging. Furthermore, investors and security analysts should not be misled by the cosmetic smoothing of accounting earnings. What we observed is hardly consonant with this view. The institutions examined hedged internally and externally, and markets developed to facilitate these activities. The link between corporate strategies and the web of markets in which they are implemented is central to an understanding of floating exchange rates and portents for the future.

Efficient markets notwithstanding, the various forms of hedging are rationally grounded in the manager's realization that borrowing (lending) opportunities and planning horizons are limited. Even if disposed toward risk neutrality, the corporate manager would be negligent in ignoring the banker's concern about the firm's exposure. In this light, hedging becomes a vehicle for husbanding net worth and managing finite lines of credit at varying interest rates. Money desk opportunities are seized as they arise. Liquidity is an overarching concern, and insolvency is a ubiquitous if shadowy threat. Finally, the conflicting interests of managers responsible for purchasing, production, marketing, and finance must be harmonized while controlling the firm's economic exposure. In limiting potential losses (gains) arising from the unpredictability of currency values, hedging serves as a substitute for financial capital in a world of incomplete and imperfect capital markets where all participants face financial constraints.

Regulations

Throughout this study, we have noted implications of financial, banking and accounting regulations and that differences among firms reflect external constraints and adaptations to them. In the United Kingdom, exchange controls and declining sterling were imperatives during most of the past decade. The earlier demise of sterling's international reserve role prompted U.K. firms to (1) deal in an expanding array of currencies; (2) accept consequent transaction exposure; (3) adopt a partially covered foreign-currency financial structure; and (4) until October 1979, effect capital flows and foreign investment under restrictive exchange regulations. U.K. firms consequently developed a keen understanding of foreign exchange exposure in both its accounting and economic dimensions. Ingenious barter financing schemes were innovated, including back-to-back, parallel loans and currency swaps. Matched foreign financing for foreign asset acquisition along with variable invoicing, inventory management, leading and lagging of payables and receivables all became weapons in the exchange risk management arsenal of U.K. firms. Public insurance programs were routinely employed, e.g., the ECGD cost-escalation cover scheme. In the closely regulated U.K. environment, the drive to understand and control exposure gave companies a lead that prepared them for the erratic exchange markets of the 1970s. Both interviews and questionnaire responses indicated an acute sensitivity among U.K. firms to the exchange risk problem as well as considerable experience in coping with it.

In the United States, exchange transactions were less regulated, and the international role of the U.S. dollar probably resulted in less exposure for American transactors. On the other hand, U.S. firms have operated within increasingly constrained regulations in banking and financial reporting in recent years. Government-sponsored export promotion programs have also differed widely, with European and Japanese governments apparently willing to adopt a more active role in export promotion than the U.S. government.[2]

FOREIGN EXCHANGE MARKETS' PERFORMANCE AND INTERNATIONAL CAPITAL MARKET INTEGRATION

Impact on Foreign Exchange Markets

The bankers interviewed indicated that flexible exchange rates and corporate hedging responses were responsible for increased trading in both spot and forward exchange markets. Under fixed exchange rates, forward currency markets were used to hedge whatever risk market participants ascribed to the central bank's commitment to official parity. Forward premiums (discounts) tended to reflect interest-rate differentials on comparable debt instruments. Covered interest arbitrage was occasionally overtaken by speculative positions anticipating imminent currency realign-

---

2 For a detailed comparison, see *Export Credit Insurance in OECD Countries* (Paris: OECD, 1979).

ments as the markets often discounted the realignments well in advance of their implementation. Such vagaries notwithstanding, companies faced with multicurrency cash flows were less concerned with day-to-day exchange-rate variations since the central bank provided at least limited protection for the official parity. Exchange risk was more often related to exchange controls and restrictions on earnings repatriation, and received limited attention as long periods of stability were punctuated by fairly predictable adjustments.

The advent of floating exchange rates launched a period of major growth in foreign exchange trading. Official figures are scant, but the Federal Reserve Bank of New York estimated daily gross turnover in New York at U.S.$10 billion to $12 billion in 1977.[3] A recent follow-up survey indicated a two and one-half-fold growth to approximately U.S.$25 billion daily gross turnover in 1980.[4] Over the same period, forward exchange trading rose from a daily volume of $3.6 billion to $10.8 billion. Almost three-fourths of the volume was spot trading, and interbank transactions accounted for over 90 percent of the turnover. The predominance of interbank trading is explained by (1) the odd maturity dates and amounts required by corporate customers; and (2) banks' reluctance to accept open currency positions overnight. Banks were thus forced to "reposition their book" constantly as markets and opportunities evolved.

Risk Bearing, Risk Shifting and Interest-Rate Arbitrage

Norman S. Fieleke has shed new light on the exposure management of U.S. banks and nonfinancial corporations.[5] His data describe net foreign exchange positions of banks and of nonbanks, and the contrast is striking. As a percentage of foreign

---

3 Roger M. Kubarych, *Foreign Exchange Markets in the United States* (Federal Reserve Bank of New York, 1978). Also see Exchange Markets Participants' Study Group, *The Foreign Exchange Markets under Floating Rates: A Study in International Finance* (New York, 1980).

4 *New York Foreign Exchange Markets Survey* (Federal Reserve Bank of New York, 1980).

5 N.S. Fieleke, "Foreign Exchange Speculation by U.S. Firms: Some New Evidence," *New England Economic Review* (1979).

activity—measured by the sum of total assets, liabilities and forward contracts outstanding—banks maintain open positions of less than 1/2 of 1 percent on average, in contrast to up to 30 percent among nonbanks. Moreover, Fieleke's statistical tests suggest that most of these corporate positions have resulted in losses.

U.S. corporations' use of forward markets to shift risk results in covered interest arbitrage effected by banks. To illustrate, consider a corporate treasurer seeking to cover a sterling payable due in three months. Depending upon the current cash position, the treasurer can (1) convert cash or cash-equivalent U.S. dollars at the current $/£ spot rate and invest the proceeds in 90-day Euro-sterling deposits; or (2) invest the U.S. dollars in the money market while purchasing a three-month sterling contract at today's forward rate. The other side of the forward transaction—the short sale of sterling—is effected by a bank. However, the bank normally will not accept this open position, even overnight. Rather, it will offset the open position by purchasing spot and selling three-month sterling. Recall that corporate/bank currency transactions are less than 10 percent of total bank currency transactions. This imbalance suggests that forward premiums (discounts) may be determined by Euro-deposit interest-rate differentials. In order to accommodate the odd dates, amounts and random arrivals of corporate bids and offers on various currencies, the banks engage in extensive interbank dealing, "swapping" deposits in different currencies in order to match the desired corporate hedge transactions, while striving to maintain a "square book." In this setting, foreign exchange dealers commonly calculate the forward premium (discount) on the basis of Euro-currency deposit interest-rate differences. To be sure, this view of Euro-currency interest-rate primacy must ultimately be reconciled with the joint determination of interest and exchange rates in a general equilibrium setting.

The volume of interbank transacting underscores the crucial role of Euro-deposit markets in risk shifting. The inevitable mismatch in trade and capital flows coupled with the banks' aversion to exchange risk and the paucity of other major risk takers in these markets explain the occasionally acute pressure on exchange rates. Thus, currency markets behave like asset markets rather than pure forward markets. A corporation's desire for cover against these vicissitudes can be understood as prudent resource

TABLE 8: AUTOCORRELATION COEFFICIENTS OF ANNUALIZED MONTH-TO-
MONTH CHANGES IN EXCHANGE-RATE MOVEMENTS AND
INTERNATIONAL INTEREST-RATE DIFFERENTIALS:
JANUARY 1972-DECEMBER 1980

	Annualized Monthly Percent Changes in Exchange Rates	Annualized Net Sum of Euro-Currency Interest-Rate Differential and Monthly Exchange-Rate Changes	Net Sum of Domestic Interest-Rate Differential and Annualized Monthly Exchange-Rate Changes
U.S.$ against £	0.06	0.06	0.06
U.S.$ against DM	− 0.06	− 0.05	− 0.06
U.S.$ against Sw. fr.	− 0.08	− 0.06	− 0.07
U.S.$ against yen	− 0.09	0.04	− 0.06
£ against DM	0.02	0.03	0.04
£ against Sw. fr.	0.06	0.10	0.10
£ against yen	0.05	0.09	0.08
DM against Sw.fr.	0.20	0.24	0.23
DM against yen	0.12	0.13	0.14
Sw.fr. against yen	− 0.04	0.03	− 0.03

*Autocorrelation coefficients measure the degree to which one month's exchange-rate
change is predictable from the prior month's change. For instance, a value of + 1.0 (or
− 1.0) would indicate total predictability; if last month's exchange-rate change for $/£ was,
for example, + 20 percent, this month's change could be predicted exactly. At the other
extreme, a coefficient of 0.0 would mean that knowledge of last month's change would be
of no value in predicting future changes.
Source: Foreign exchange data courtesy of National Westminster Bank Ltd.

conservation permitting management to focus on other business
considerations. In the longer run, purchasing power parity will
restore exchange rates to relationships dictated by inflation differentials. However, abrupt fluctuations around these equilibria
have been common since 1971.

Evidence of systematic movements in short-run exchange rates
is shown in Table 8. The autocorrelation coefficient measures the
degree to which one month's exchange-rate change is predictable
from the prior month's change. Also, given what has been said
about covered interest-rate arbitrage and the resulting determina-
tion of forward exchange premiums (discounts) by interest-rate differentials, it is useful to examine the sum of the interest-rate differential and the exchange-rate changes in testing for autocorrela-

tion. Most of the coefficients shown are statistically significant.[6] Foreign exchange market efficiency has been extensively studied, and it would be presumptuous to conclude that these markets are inefficient on the basis of our fragmentary evidence.[7] However, the covering of foreign exchange risk—probably amplified by book exposure hedging and tax considerations—may explain the dramatic recent growth in forward exchange trading. Some exchange-rate smoothing might be possible by opening currency markets to wider participation. Exchange markets are presently dominated by world class banks who studiously avoid sustained open positions. A more open and organized futures market, free of government intervention, might smooth exchange-rate fluctuations. Even though entry of speculators would not ensure reduced exchange-rate volatility, it may be presumed that a well capitalized and independently acting base of speculators would dampen exchange-rate fluctuations.

Macro Adjustments: Cause or Effect

Prior to 1971, many economists advocated a laissez-faire exchange-rate system to avoid the unseemly shifting of wealth from central banks to speculators as asymmetric market expectations were ultimately validated. Advocates of freely floating exchange rates averred that unimpeded speculation would be stabilizing, and freed from the necessity to support exchange parity, monetary authorities would have greater freedom to pursue domestic stabilization objectives. Further, with sufficient export and import elasticities, trade imbalances would be expeditiously rectified. Similarly, interest-rate disparities would rationally direct capital flows.

Trade and Capital Flows

Sluggish and asymmetric price adjustments in import and export markets cause the so-called J curve effect. No less important is the price pass-through phenomenon facilitated by oligopolistic

---

6 In not more than 1 chance in 10 could a coefficient large enough to be deemed significant arise purely from chance.

7 For example, see J. Frenkel, *"Flexible Exchange Rates in the Seventies,"* Working Paper #450, National Bureau of Economic Research (February 1980).

goods market structures. The net effect is a constricted trade account response to exchange-rate movements. These limited adjustments seem to have aggravated inflation and expedited its transmission across national boundaries. There is certainly little in recent U.K. and U.S experience to suggest that exchange-rate volatility, trade imbalances and inflation are ephemeral phenomena.

Indeed, much of the recent academic literature maintains that partial balance—trade, current or capital—has no significance in itself.[8] The monetary approach to the balance of payments contends that observed flows are gradual adjustments to desired stocks of financial assets that each nation seeks to accumulate. When desired stocks—which are influenced by prices, interest and exchange rates—are attained, the flows terminate. Any change in prices and/or rates determines a new equilibrium leading to the resumption of asset flows. This view abstracts from the feedback effects of corporate responses on trade and capital flows.

Exchange rate-based corporate behavior, described in the previous chapter, helps to explain recent capital account behavior. Our discussion of the liability adjustments for long-term hedging (back-to-back or parallel loans) indicated a tendency to reduce the debt-equity ratio to deal with noncontractual exposure. To the extent that this behavior is reflected in financing decisions and capital budgeting for foreign investments, it may alter long-term capital flows, both direct and portfolio. Overall, higher capital costs for the firm could be expected. Limited evidence is found in the higher hurdle rates used for foreign investment decisions under flexible exchange rates, although factors such as higher inflation rates and inflation risk may have been as important in raising hurdle rates.

From the viewpoint of the official reserve account, exchange-rate volatility has two important effects. First, the risk of ignoring the payments problem is heightened. Second, volatility increases the need for foreign currency reserves. A useful parallel can be drawn between corporate and central bank reactions to managed floating. In both cases, exchange-rate volatility prompted increased holdings of liquid assets, i.e., reserves to cushion earnings

---

8 Among the literature is International Monetary Fund, *The Monetary Approach to the Balance of Payments* (Washington, D.C., 1977).

TABLE 9: RESERVE USE AND THE EXCHANGE-RATE REGIME
(Average Absolute Values of the Monthly
Percentage Changes in Reserves)

	Jan. 1965- July 1971	Aug. 1971- Dec. 1971	Jan. 1972- Feb. 1973	Mar. 1973- Mar. 1980
U.S.	0.835	3.920	1.296	0.407
Canada	0.145	1.076	1.271	1.273
Japan	1.249	10.163	0.320	0.853
Austria	0.013	1.018	0.267	0.275
Belgium	0.049	2.912	0.285	0.661
Denmark	0.663	6.951	0.827	0.548
France	0.416	2.068	0.091	0.142
Germany	0.599	2.101	1.501	0.278
Italy	0.059	1.780	2.327	0.880
Netherlands	0.019	2.250	0.871	0.087
Norway	0.855	1.499	0.665	0.690
Sweden	0.418	1.768	1.960	0.050
Switzerland	0.112	5.988	0.831	0.370
U.K.	0.710	5.075	4.262	1.015
All industrial countries*	0.083	0.447	0.328	0.278

*Includes countries other than those shown.
Source: IMF data as presented in *The Money Manager,* November 24, 1980.

fluctuations in the former case and trade and capital account deficits in the latter. The central banks ostensibly seek to mitigate adjustment costs associated with short-term exchange-rate volatility. Market intervention aimed at smoothing exchange rates requires reserves or credit (swap) lines. The upshot has been larger official reserve holdings and greater intervention under floating exchange rates. The greater volatility of official reserves is illustrated in Table 9.

Internationalization of Credit Creation and Inflation

Floating exchange rates seem to have tightened the links between national and international money markets and consequently quickened the transmission of monetary disturbances across national borders. Although not a direct result of floating exchange rates, this integration has been fostered by them and by corporate responses thereto. The growth of Euro-markets has stimulated and has been stimulated by the need for forward cover. Corporate requirements create a steady two-way flow of currencies that provides liquidity to the offshore money markets through which these flows are channeled.

The widely discussed spillover effect of Euro-markets into domestic markets has tended to internationalize the credit creation process. Coupled with inflation ratcheting, these spillover effects have probably increased the international transmission of monetary disturbances and inflation. The dramatic Euro-market growth that has accelerated since the early 1970s is a most unlikely coincidence. The widespread use of the Euro-market by corporations and central banks for funding and hedging has spurred this growth beyond what would have been anticipated on the basis of energy price increases alone. This suggests still another indirect cost of floating exchange rates.

Pricing Decisions and Pass-Through Inflation
In our survey, we found that flexible exchange rates had limited impact on pricing decisions. Nevertheless, the international transmission of inflation seems to have been facilitated by floating rates. This suggests downward price inflexibility, price ratcheting or another systemic rigidity since inflation differentials are offset by exchange-rate adjustments, according to the theory of purchasing power parity. The experience in key manufacturing industries, e.g., automobiles and household appliances, suggests an explanation. As import prices rose with the decline of the U.S. dollar and sterling, domestic industries might have exploited widening domestic price advantages over imports. However, many manufactures are produced in concentrated industries with some price-setting capability. Domestic producers often find it profitable to follow the price adjustments initiated by foreign producers. This acceptance of foreign price leadership subverts the classical adjustment mechanism. The domestic producer transmits inflationary impulses. Over longer periods, of course, the depreciation itself leads to domestic inflation as domestic input prices are bid up in response to higher import prices. This parallels the fixed-rate situation where the gains from devaluing are inflated away.

BEYOND MARKET ADJUSTMENTS:
CORPORATE STRUCTURE AND FUNCTION

Markets Versus Corporate Structure

The mismatch in the timing of receivables and payables is the major source of exchange risk for many corporations. For instance, the cost of goods sold may be denominated in a base currency, say U.S. dollars, while sales are invoiced in another, say sterling, thereby exposing the firm's transactions to U.S. dollar/sterling exchange-rate variations over the life of the receivables. The longer their life, the greater the potential risk. Internal solutions, such as leading or lagging payments, changes in the invoicing currency, price adjustment clauses, and inventory valuation adjustments, do not require market intermediation. Hence, risk is managed either internally, with attendant managerial cost, or externally, with a combination of managerial and transaction costs. These practices were documented in the three countries considered here.

Beyond the risk of current and contractual flows, we encounter a more amorphous form of exposure which is less readily dissipated. *Translation* exposure arises as the firm acquires operating assets abroad and assumes foreign currency-denominated liabilities. Hedging the balance sheet is no longer a straightforward problem. Denomination and maturity mismatching among assets and liabilities creates exchange-rate exposure. Both positive and negative cash flows are committed in a variety of currencies. Some of these cash flows are known in timing and in amounts, whereas others are uncertain and often affected by exchange rates that are not known.

The corporation is exposed to cash flow variations arising from its longer-term operating commitments. The most basic exposure is to changes in future costs, sales and earnings streams resulting from exchange-rate variability. This exposure depends on the properties of the markets in which the firm conducts its business. Exposure varies with the mix of inputs used and outputs produced by the firm and properties of the markets in which these inputs and outputs are traded. This noncontractual exposure is rooted in the dependency of input-output mixes, quantity flows and relative prices on exchange rates. These complex uncertainties are not readily amenable to dissipation through hedging because the magnitudes of exposed flows are themselves uncertain. Contractual exposure usually involves translating the value of known quantities into some base *numéraire*. The core of uncertainty is limited to the exchange rate between the *numéraire* and the foreign unit of account. Noncontractual exposure involves uncertainty regarding the exchange rate as well as the physical quantities to be valued. For example, exchange-rate variation will affect foreign demand for a corporation's goods as well as the value at which such sales are translated into U.S. dollars. This risk is not readily shifted or dissipated using routine hedging techniques.

Our survey indicated that MNCs sustained additional exposure as a result of exchange-rate volatility. Greater international diversification may diffuse some of this risk. Although noncontractual exposure is rarely mentioned as a motive for international diversification, it has probably intensified the currency diversification of multinationals, and further geographic dispersion of the MNC can be anticipated. This may explain why firms reported little adverse impact from floating rates on their direct foreign investment. Ultimately, as MNCs' direct investments and markets become more internationally diffused, the home currency could become an object of choice rather than an accident of history. Hedging would then assume an added dimension as the MNC transcends its national origin. The new transnational corporation could be expected to pursue shareholders' welfare by choosing the most stable medium in which to value its assets.

The Firm's Capital Structure as a Hedging Vehicle

Facing uncertainty as to the timing and magnitude of cash flows, the corporation can find only limited help in forward markets. Hence, much of the balance sheet exposure must be controlled internally. The elusive ideal is a perfectly matched maturity and denomination structure of assets and liabilities. However, a piecemeal or partial approach is typical.

One alternative is to reduce debt in favor of equity. This tendency is seen in the survey through the preference for currency swaps over other financing arrangements. Variations on this financing approach all emphasize covering exposure without increasing the debt-equity ratio. These developments illustrate a potentially important implication of the uncertainty arising from floating exchange rates. Firms substituting equity for debt arguably face an increased cost of capital. This is one dimension of the cost of risk assumption by firms operating in imperfect capital markets. The domestic analog is the effect of inflation in depressing equity markets. Alternatively, if all assets and liabilities are translated at current rates, the firm may be induced to hedge its foreign currency-denominated asset position with foreign currency liabilities. Indeed, foreign financing alternatives were cited by the firms surveyed as a favored means of hedging long-term exposure in a depreciation-prone currency.

The potential for the use of local capital markets varies from country to country. Here again, as in the foreign exchange/money markets, the development of the Euro-bond market has proved invaluable. Unencumbered debt markets are clearly one of the keys to cost-effective hedging. In short-term markets, covered interest arbitrage intermediated by exchange markets provides liquid forward markets for hedging exchange risk. Similarly, the ability to issue long-term debt in a variety of currencies, via the Euro-bond market, is a key to hedging long-term exchange risk. The process of risk transfer requires interconnected debt markets if financial intermediaries are to maintain forward currency markets. The centrality of offshore capital markets in risk-transfer activities is not unrelated to their success in transcending public regulation.

The maturity structure of debt is yet another consideration in the hedging of exchange risk. The adjustment of bond interest rates to inflation is often slow and variable, and inflation-adjusted returns therefore tend to vary internationally. Charts 5 through 7 illustrate the volatility and country-to-country variations in selected short- and long-term interest rates. The sluggishness of bond interest rates in impounding inflation levels is illustrated in Chart 8. Exchange markets seem to reflect diverse inflationary trends and expected exchange-rate changes more quickly than do long-term bond markets.

To the extent that short- and long-term liabilities are translated differently, the firm may have a maturity preference for hedging purposes. For instance, if current exchange rates are used for both long- and short-term debt, then the former would be preferred for a devaluation-prone currency as the interest rate will be abnormally low in view of the inflation rate. A revolving Euro-loan

CHART 5:   SHORT-TERM INTEREST RATES
(Percent per Annum)

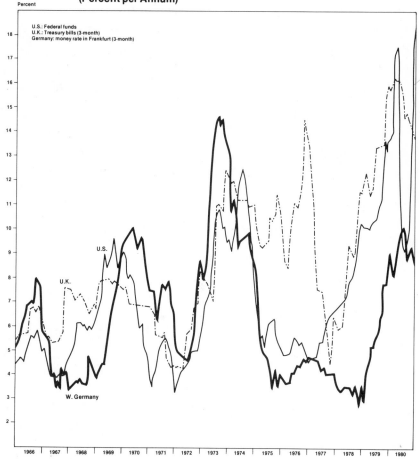

Source: IMF, *International Financial Statistics Yearbook.*

with a LIBOR-based floating rate would not be as inflation-proof.

Asset Structure

Most nonfinancial firms have limited flexibility in adjusting assets for hedging purposes. The fixity of plant and technology and even short-term asset requirements restrict the scope of asset restructuring. The firm's operating assets are often akin to an ex-

CHART 6:   EURO-CURRENCY INTEREST RATES
(Percent per Annum)

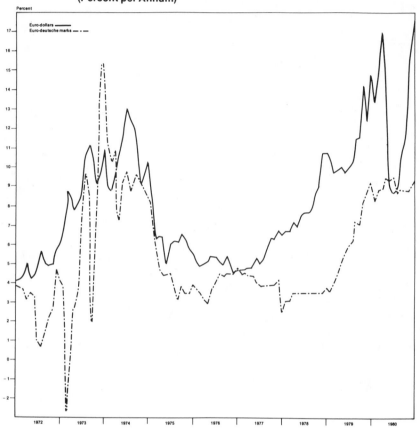

Source: National Westminster Bank.

ogenously dictated constraint. The burden of adjustment thus falls most heavily on the liability side. In principle, however, shortening the term-to-maturity of assets is possible, and often desirable. U.S. accounting conventions, as embodied in the original FASB No. 8, tend to offset such an inclination by mandating the translation of fixed assets at historic rates and current assets (except inventories) at current rates. To the extent that the U.K. and Canadian translation rules allow greater flexibility, the effect of exchange-rate volatility on asset composition should be more pronounced and hence more discernible. FASB No. 8 illustrates how accounting conventions can create incentives for

CHART 7: LONG-TERM INTEREST RATES
(Percent per Annum)

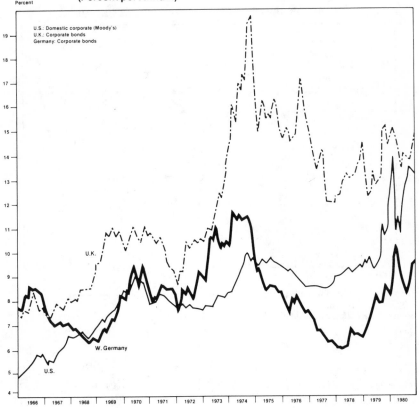

Source: Morgan Guaranty Trust Company of New York, *World Financial Markets.*

cosmetic hedging with inevitable costs. Another example, cited in interviews, was to lease to remove fixed assets from the balance sheet.

Organizational Adjustments

Our survey showed that changes in corporate structure and the loci of decisionmaking responsibility within the corporation were part of the adjustment to more volatile exchange rates. Short-run hedging strategies clearly lead to well-defined responsibilities and the expansion of the international corporate finance function. In

CHART 8: DIFFERENCES BETWEEN BOND YIELDS AND INFLATION RATES (Percent Per Annum)*

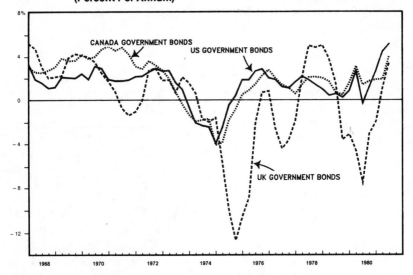

*The data measure the yield to maturity on long-term government bonds minus the annual inflation rates for each country.
Source: International Bond Market Research, Salomon Brothers.

view of the exchange-rate implications for capital structure and asset selection, long-run implications may be even more important. Long-run hedging strategies are so far-reaching that they are likely to elevate further the finance function in overall corporate planning. This elevation is likely to be expressed in increased personnel and staffing commitments. These organizational changes are still emerging and are likely to become more pronounced. Moreover, the expanded global exposure of the MNC probably means that exchange risk, and most especially noncontractual exposure, will be a centralizing force within the multinational.

Improving Risk Management

Exchange risk is unavoidable under fixed or floating rates. Under the floating rate system extant since 1971, however, the volatility of exchange rates has been demonstrably greater. Chapter II described the privatization of exchange risk management. The earlier fixed exchange-rate system partially ensured the conversion rate of cash flows at the expense of government-maintained foreign exchange reserves and constraints on domestic stabilization policy. It is arguable whether the private risk-transfer costs exceed the public costs of risk bearing through pegged rates. But the distribution or incidence of these costs is clearly different. Under the prevailing system, the costs become part of the MNCs' operating expenses whereas previously costs were more widely shared by society. The rationale for this wider sharing of costs was found in the government's putative responsibility for maintaining a stable backdrop for economic intercourse, as illustrated by governmental roles in the enforcement of private contracts and management of the domestic money stock. Governmental disparities in trade, nontariff regulations and tax and export guarantee programs influence the distribution of foreign exchange risk. Some corporations face aggravated exposure whereas others are practically insulated from it. Furthermore, governmental interventions in exchange markets are not determined exclusively on the basis of exchange rates or market efficiency considerations. For example, foreign exchange markets in Germany are used in the implementation of monetary policy for domestic stabilization purposes. In our world of second-best solutions, intervention in exchange markets may be preferable to the practical alternatives of exchange controls and similar restrictions.

Thus, we feel sure that exchange risk management will remain a formidable challenge to managers of corporate resources. Moreover, risk transfer must ultimately involve foreign exchange money and capital markets. The need for efficient facilities is illustrated by the Euro-markets' facile handling of the enormous financial flows of recent years. Misguided attempts to regulate these markets would probably increase the cost and complexity of risk transfer and even jeopardize the smooth functioning of a mechanism that is essential to enable international business to cope with the challenges of floating exchange rates.

APPENDIX 1
The Questionnaire

I. DEFINING AND MEASURING FOREIGN EXCHANGE RISK

International business operations involve cash flows and financial statements denominated in a variety of currencies. Fluctuations in exchange rates sensitize the parent company's reported financial condition, tax liability and long-term liability. Consequently, exchange risk is perceived differently by accountants, managers, shareholders, and government regulators.

Reporting

1. (a) For reporting purposes, does your company use

_____ the FASB No. 8 standards (for U.S. companies)?
_____ other? If so, check the appropriate space below for each major balance sheet item and explain:

Item	Translation Basis		
	Current	**Historic**	**Other**
Fixed assets	_____	_____	_____
Current assets	_____	_____	_____
Inventories	_____	_____	_____
Short-term liabilities	_____	_____	_____
Long-term liabilities	_____	_____	_____
Equity	_____	_____	_____

   (b) Explain the underlying rationale for accounting policies. That is, indicate the constraints that delimit your choice and the reasons for choosing among available methods.

2. (a) For internal management purposes, does your company adjust accounting exposure figures to account for "economic exposure," i.e., exchange-rate exposure of expected future cash flows?

_____ yes   _____ no

   (b) If you answered yes to question 2 (a), describe the adjustments you carry out to arrive at a measure of economic exposure.

II. OBJECTIVES AND STRATEGIES OF EXCHANGE RISK MANAGEMENT

Objectives

3. Among the following possible objectives of exchange risk management, which one would have the highest priority in your company?

_____ minimize earnings fluctuations due to foreign exchange risk
_____ preserve the cash-flow generating power of foreign operations
_____ avoid major foreign exchange losses
_____ provide balance sheet protection
_____ reduce net accounting exposure
_____ reduce net economic exposure
_____ maximize home currency equivalent of foreign income
_____ some combination of the above or other (please explain)

4. How does your company distribute responsibility for foreign exchange risk management? That is, describe the degree to which such responsibilities are centralized at the head office or dispersed among operating units and/or subsidiaries.

5. (a) How has the staffing of the foreign exchange risk management function changed in recent years? (Please comment on both the qualitative and quantitative aspects of staffing. Estimate orders of magnitude, if at all possible.)

   (b) How have information and reporting systems adjusted to new problems posed by floating exchange rates? (Cost or quantity estimates would be most helpful.)

   (c) Estimate the total resource cost (in dollars or pounds or percentage change) of foreign exchange risk management efforts by your company in 1970, 1975 and 1979.

Internal Risk Handling

6. What currency is used in invoicing intercompany transactions?

   _____ the parent's
   _____ the subsidiary's
   _____ a third-country currency
   _____ other; explain

7. What currency is used in invoicing external transactions?

   _____ the company's
   _____ the client's
   _____ a third-country currency
   _____ a currency particular to your product
   _____ other; explain

8. How has foreign exchange-rate volatility affected your company's pricing policies?

   (a) How has the frequency of price adjustments been affected?

   (b) How important are the administrative costs of more frequent price adjustments?

   (c) How has exchange-rate volatility affected your ability or willingness to quote fixed prices for future deliveries?

   (d) Has the locus of responsibility for pricing decisions shifted within the firm as a result of increased exchange-rate volatility? If so, please explain.

9. How has exchange-rate volatility affected your company's

   (a) timing of invoicing?
   (b) terms of payment?

External Risk Shifting

10. How regularly and completely does your company hedge its transaction exposure?

	As Completely as Possible	Partially	Not at All
_____ (Almost) Always			
_____ Seldom			
_____ Never			

11. How regularly and completely does your company hedge its translation exposure?

	As Completely as Possible	Partially	Not at All
_____ (Almost) Always			
_____ Seldom			
_____ Never			

12. If you attempt to hedge translation exposure, briefly explain why.

13. What short-term hedging vehicle does your company rely on mostly?

    _____ forward markets, if available
    _____ money markets
    _____ overseas finance companies and other invoicing vehicles
    _____ other; explain

14. In evaluating long-term hedging strategies, does your company

    _____ adjust the capitalization of overseas subsidiaries?
    _____ evaluate alternative local versus parent company currency-financing schemes?
    _____ rely on exchange-rate forecasts to compare alternative financing schemes?
    _____ other; explain

15. In effecting long-term hedging, does your company use

    _____ foreign currency-denominated debt instruments?
    _____ parallel, swap or back-to-back loans?
    _____ long-term forward contracts, when available?
    _____ other; explain

16. Decisionmaking in the exchange-rate realm can be arbitrarily decomposed as follows:

    (a) general policy formulation (statement of objectives)

(b) (1) analysis of internal and external data
    (2) development of forecasts
(c) decisions regarding the degree to which the company's various types of exposure should be hedged
(d) development and implementation of hedging policies in light of (c)

Explain how your company implements each of the above steps. That is, describe how responsibility for the above is distributed within your company.

Inventory Management

17. Has the level of foreign currency-denominated inventories been changed as a result of flexible rates?

18. How has the management of inventories been affected by flexible exchange rates?

Investment

19. Apart from inventories, how has the foreign investment/foreign asset acquisition decision been changed by floating exchange rates?

III. COMPANY CHARACTERISTICS

20. In which industry do you consider your company to be?

21. What were your company's 1978 sales?

22. What percentage of total sales is foreign sales?

23. What is the asset size of your company?

24. What percentage of total assets is foreign assets?

25. List the major foreign currencies in which your company has exposure.

26. In how many countries do you have productive operations?

27. In how many countries do you have sales?

28. In how many countries do you have revenues?

APPENDIX 2
Responses to the Questionnaire

Exhibit numbers correspond to question numbers in Appendix 1. All tabular numbers have been rounded. The term "forex" means foreign exchange.

EXHIBIT 1(a): ACCOUNTING PRACTICES

			Respondents					
	Total	%	U.S.	%	U.K.	%	Can.	%
FASB No. 8	12	44	10	91	1[b]	8	1	33
Other*	15	56	1[a]	9	12	92	2	67
	27	100	11	100	13	100	3	100

*These responses are tabulated on the next page in Exhibit 1(a) continued.

[a] A bank transferred some nonmonetary balance sheet items (deferred costs, prepaid expenses, goodwill) in current terms.

[b] From a U.K. subsidiary of a U.S. firm.

EXHIBIT 1(b): REASONS FOR PRESENT ACCOUNTING PRACTICES

	Respondents	%
Accuracy of current valuation	6	22
Application simplicity	2	7
Most widely accepted in U.K.	2	7
U.K. companies act	1	4
U.K. accounting standards	2	7
Stock Exchange requirements	1	4
	14	51

EXHIBIT 1(a) continued

Balance Sheet Item	Translation Basis*																								
	Current								Historic								Other								
	Respondents								Respondents								Respondents								
	Total	%	U.S.	%	U.K.	%	Can.	%	Total	%	U.S.	%	U.K.¹	%	Can.	%	Total	%	U.S.	%	U.K.	%	Can.	%
Fixed assets	10	69	0	0	10	67	0	0	6	40	2	13	2	13	2	13	0	0	0	0	0	0	0	0
Current assets	15	100	2	13	11	73	2	13	1	7	0	0	1	7	0	0	0	0	0	0	0	0	0	0
Inventories	11	73	0	0	9	60	2	13	3	20	1	7	2	13	0	0	0	0	0	0	0	0	0	0
Short-term liabilities	15	100	2	13	11	73	2	13	1	7	0	0	1	7	0	0	0	0	0	0	0	0	0	0
Long-term liabilities²	12	80	2	13	10	67	0	0	3	20	0	0	1	7	2	13	0	0	0	0	0	0	0	0
Equity²	10	67	0	0	10	67	0	0	4	27	1	7	1	7	2	13	1	7	1	7	0	0	0	0

*Responses on this exhibit offer a breakdown of the translation basis only for those firms (15) that indicated that they followed an accounting method different from FASB No. 8.

¹ One U.K. firm used historic costs for all but internal reports; another used historic costs in valuing fixed assets and inventories for S.E.C. reporting purposes.

² One U.K. firm answered "not applicable."

EXHIBIT 2: INTERNAL ADJUSTMENTS TO ACCOUNT FOR ECONOMIC EXPOSURE

(a) Does Your Company Adjust?

	Respondents							
	Total	%	U.S.	%	U.K.	%	Can.	%
Yes	8	30	5	46	2	15	1	33
No	19	70	6	55	11	85	2	67
	27	100	11	100	13	100	3	100

(b) Kinds of Adjustments

	Respondents	%
U.S.		
Include inventories in overall exposure	3	27
Hedge nontaxable income overseas	1	9
Hedge interest receivable and payable	1	9
Adjust figures based on ability of international subsidiaries to change prices	1	9
Adjust forecasts for forex gains and losses in foreign operations	1	9
Adjust intercompany balances	1	9
	8	72
U.K.		
Evaluate cash flows, forex risk and necessary price monthly	1	8
Profit and leverage effects of forex risk	1	8
	2	16
Canada		
No FASB No. 8 adjustments but separate cash flow and exchange transactions adjustment	1	33

EXHIBIT 3: FOREX RISK MANAGEMENT OBJECTIVES

	Total	%	U.S. Subtotal	%	Single	%	Multiple	%	U.K. Subtotal	%	Single	%	Multiple	%	Canada Subtotal	%	Single	%	Multiple	%
Minimize earnings fluctuations	5	11	3	14	0	0	3	18	2	10	1	13	1	8	0	0	0	0	0	0
Preserve cash-flow generation	2	4	1	5	0	0	1	6	0	0	0	0	0	0	1	25	1	50	0	0
Avoid major forex losses	15	33	6	29	2	50	4	24	8	40	3	38	5	42	1	25	1	50	0	0
Provide balance sheet protection	4	9	2	10	0	0	2	12	2	10	2	25	0	0	0	0	0	0	0	0
Reduce net accounting exposure	2	4	1	5	0	0	1	6	1	5	0	0	1	8	0	0	0	0	0	0
Reduce net economic exposure	12	27	7	33	2	50	5	29	4	20	2	25	2	17	1	25	0	0	1	50
Maximize home currency equivalent income	5	11	1	5	0	0	1	6	3	15	0	0	3	25	1	25	0	0	1	50
	45	100	21	100	4	100	17	100	20	100	8	100	12	100	4	100	2	100	2	100

Respondents

EXHIBIT 4: DISTRIBUTION OF FOREX RISK MANAGEMENT RESPONSIBILITY

	Total	%	U.S.	%	U.K.	%	Can.	%
				Respondents				
Centralized forex management with corporate policy set for exposure of subsidiaries	9	33	6	55	1	8	2	67
Forex policy set centrally; subsidiaries implement policies independently and are responsible for profit and loss performance	8	30	3	27	5	39	0	0
Centralized policy with input of recommendations from subsidiaries	2	7	2	18	0	0	0	0
Consolidated cash flows and exposure, corporation responsibility; local cash flows and exposure, subsidiary responsibility	3	11	0	0	2	15	1	33
Mutual agreement between parent and subsidiary	1	4	0	0	1	8	0	0
Decentralized with coordination from central office if necessary	4	15	0	0	4	31	0	0
	27	100	11	100	13	100	3	100

EXHIBIT 5(a): STAFFING CHANGES

	Respondents							
	Total	%	U.S.	%	U.K.	%	Can.	%
No significant change	9	33	4	36	4	31	1	33
Forex trading staff size and quality increased; head office not as much	3	11	2	18	1	8	0	0
Tenfold increase in forex centers in head office and field	1	4	0	0	1	8	0	0
Increased staff	1	4	0	0	1	8	0	0
Quality increase in staff; no personnel increase	1	4	0	0	0	0	1	33
Increase in quality information from subsidiaries	1	4	0	0	1	8	0	0
More involvement of financial management (time)	5	19	2	18	2	15	1	33
More involvement and specialization of subsidiary exposure management	1	4	1	9	0	0	0	0
More senior management involvement; one specialist added	1	4	0	0	1	8	0	0
More time and expertise in existing staff; no personnel increase	1	4	1	9	0	0	0	0
More central policy adherence, delegation of forex responsibility and use of outside consultants	1	4	1	9	0	0	0	0
Computer model and forex committee added	1	4	0	0	1	8	0	0
Not applicable	1	4	0	0	1	8	0	0
	27	100	11	100	13	100	3	100

EXHIBIT 5(b): INFORMATION AND REPORTING SYSTEM ADJUSTMENTS

	Respondents							
	Total	%	U.S.	%	U.K.	%	Can.	%
No change	4	15	1	9	2	15	1	33
Normal evolutionary change	5	19	2	18	3	23	0	0
New system to calculate exposure	3	11	2	18	0	0	1	33
New system of data flow; more accurate information in reporting system	1	4	1	9	0	0	0	0
Monthly exposure reporting system; quarterly senior management review; budgeted vs. actual results; monthly review	1	4	1	9	0	0	0	0
Advisory services and computer packages	1	4	1	9	0	0	0	0
Efforts to define exposure, set up reporting system and act in response to forex conditions	1	4	1	9	0	0	0	0
Additional reporting and monitoring systems	2	7	1	9	1	8	0	0
Creation of profit center attached to bond department	1	4	1	9	0	0	0	0
Systematic and continual evaluation of forex and cash flow	1	4	0	0	1	8	0	0
Creation of forex committee, inhouse models and use of advisory services	1	4	0	0	1	8	0	0
Sensitivity analysis of effect of currency fluctuations	1	4	0	0	1	8	0	0
Computerization; risk minimization; profit-taking	1	4	0	0	1	8	0	0
Computer addition; forex computer model; forex committee; continual forward monitoring (short and medium term); inhouse money and forex dealers (note: a large corporation)	1	4	0	0	1	8	0	0
Subsidiaries phoned when exposure risks are high (U.K. subsidiary of U.S. firm)	1	4	0	0	1	8	0	0
Improved information and reporting systems	1	4	0	0	0	0	1	33
Unknown	1	4	0	0	1	8	0	0
	27	100	11	100	13	100	3	100

EXHIBIT 5(c): ABSOLUTE OR PERCENT COST CHANGE OF FOREX RISK MANAGEMENT EFFORTS IN 1970, 1975 AND 1979

	Total	%	U.S.	%	U.K.	%	Can.	%
					Respondents			
No change	2	7	1	9	1	8	0	0
Not significant	3	11	1	9	1	8	1	33
Some increase	2	7	2	18	0	0	0	0
Negligible overall; 20% for central finance department	1	4	0	0	1	8	0	0
1975, much increase; 1979, no change	1	4	1	9	0	0	0	0
Progressive increase first 5 yrs.; substantial increase afterwards	1	4	0	0	1	8	0	0
Percent changes (1975-79)								
5-15	1	4	1	9	0	0	0	0
25-100	1	4	0	0	1	8	0	0
50-75	1	4	1	9	0	0	0	0
54-117	1	4	0	0	0	0	1	33
75-128	1	4	1	9	0	0	0	0
100-200	1	4	1	9	0	0	0	0
200-900	1	4	1	9	0	0	0	0
15-20 (real terms)	1	4	0	0	1	8	0	0
Quantity costs (1970, '75 and '79)								
0, 0 and £20,000	1	4	0	0	1	8	0	0
0, £20,000 and £10,000	1	4	0	0	1	8	0	0
£20,000, £50,000 and £100,000	1	4	0	0	1	8	0	0
Not available/quantifiable	5	19	1	9	4	31	0	0
No response	1	4	0	0	0	0	1	33
	27	100	11	100	13	100	3	100

EXHIBIT 6: CURRENCY USED IN INVOICING INTERCOMPANY TRANSACTIONS

	\multicolumn{8}{c}{Respondents}						
	Total	%	U.S.	%	U.K.	%	Can.	%
(a) Parent's	9	33	6	55	2	15	1	33
(b) Subsidiary's	0	0	0	0	0	0	0	0
(c) Third country's	2	7	0	0	1	8	1	33
(d) Other								
Nonspecific	3	11	2	18	1	8	0	0
(a) and (b)	3	11	2	18	1	8	0	0
(a), (b) and (c)	3	11	0	0	3	23	0	0
Exporting country's	1	4	1	9	0	0	0	0
Exporting country's or U.S.								
$, if no market for exporting currency	1	4	0	0	1	8	0	0
Bank customer's	1	4	0	0	1	8	0	0
Billing country's	1	4	0	0	1	8	0	0
Intercompany transactions insignificant	1	4	0	0	1	8	0	0
No subsidiaries outside home country	1	4	0	0	0	0	1	33
Not applicable	1	4	0	0	1	8	0	0
	27	100	11	100	13	100	3	100

EXHIBIT 7: CURRENCY USED IN INVOICING EXTERNAL TRANSACTIONS

	\multicolumn{8}{c}{Respondents}						
	Total	%	U.S.	%	U.K.	%	Can.	%
(a) Company's	3	11	3	27	0	0	0	0
(b) Client's (defined as local currency)	2	7	0	0	2	15	0	0
(c) Third country's	1	4	0	0	1	8	0	0
(d) Currency particular to product	2	7	0	0	1	8	1	33
(e) Other								
Most currency of bank unit involved	1	4	1	9	0	0	0	0
(a) and (b)	4	15	3	27	0	0	1	33
(a), (b) and (c)	5	19	1	9	4	31	0	0
(b) and (c)	1	4	0	0	1	8	0	0
(b) and (d)	1	4	1	9	0	0	0	0
(a) and subsidiary's	1	4	1	9	0	0	0	0
(d) and exporting country's	1	4	0	0	1	8	0	0
Currency taker's (b), (c) and (d)	1	4	0	0	0	0	1	33
Whichever appropriate	2	7	0	0	2	15	0	0
Not applicable	1	4	1	9	0	0	0	0
No response	1	4	0	0	1	8	0	0
	27	100	11	100	13	100	3	100

EXHIBIT 8: EFFECTS OF FOREIGN EXCHANGE-RATE VOLATILITY ON PRICING POLICIES

(a) Effect on Frequency of Price Adjustments

	Respondents							
	Total	%	U.S.	%	U.K.	%	Can.	%
Not significant	9	33	4	36	5	39	0	0
A little increase	7	26	2	18	3	23	2	67
Much increase	4	15	2	18	1	8	1	33
Not applicable	7	26	3	27	4	31	0	0
	27	100	11	100	13	100	3	100

(b) Importance of Administrative Costs of More Frequent Price Adjustments

	Respondents							
	Total	%	U.S.	%	U.K.	%	Can.	%
Not significant	18	67	7	64	9	69	2	67
Substantial	2	7	1	9	1	8	0	0
Not applicable	7	26	3	27	3	23	1	33
	27	100	11	100	13	100	3	100

(c) Effect on Fixed-Price Contracts

	Respondents							
	Total	%	U.S.	%	U.K.	%	Can.	%
Not significant	14	52	6	55	7	54	1	33
Increase in home country currency used in fixed-price contracts	1	4	1	9	0	0	0	0
More caution with foreign currency quotes	1	4	0	0	0	0	1	33
Escalation clauses	3	11	1	9	2	15	0	0
Conversion clauses	2	7	0	0	1	8	1	33
Not applicable	6	22	3	27	3	23	0	0
	27	100	11	100	13	100	3	100

(d) Shift in Locus of Pricing Decisions

	Respondents							
	Total	%	U.S.	%	U.K.	%	Can.	%
No	15	56	5	46	8	62	2	67
Yes								
Some shift to corporate management	4	15	2	18	2	15	0	0
More local control	1	4	1	9	0	0	0	0
Not applicable	7	26	3	27	3	23	1	33
	27	100	11	100	13	100	3	100

EXHIBIT 9: EFFECTS OF FOREX-RATE VOLATILITY ON INVOICING AND TERMS OF PAYMENT

(a) On Invoice Timing

	Respondents							
	Total	%	U.S.	%	U.K.	%	Can.	%
None	17	63	5	46	9	69	3	100
Very little	2	7	0	0	2	15	0	0
Varies	1	4	1	9	0	0	0	0
Greater use of progress payments, intercompany and third party	1	4	1	9	0	0	0	0
Intercompany transactions only	1	4	1	9	0	0	0	0
Not applicable	5	19	3	27	2	15	0	0
	27	100	11	100	13	100	3	100

(b) On Terms of Payment

	Respondents							
	Total	%	U.S.	%	U.K.	%	Can.	%
None	16	59	6	55	7	54	3	100
Very little	2	7	0	0	2	15	0	0
Varies from country to country	1	4	1	9	0	0	0	0
Hedge via contracts or market	1	4	0	0	1	8	0	0
Intercompany transaction (lead/lag device)	1	4	1	9	0	0	0	0
Tightened	1	4	0	0	1	8	0	0
Not applicable	5	19	3	27	2	15	0	0
	27	100	11	100	13	100	3	100

EXHIBIT 10: REGULARITY OF HEDGING TRANSACTION EXPOSURE

Frequency*	As completely as possible								Partially								Not applicable
Degree**	Total	%	U.S.	%	U.K.	%	Can.	%	Total	%	U.S.	%	U.K.	%	Can.	%	
(Almost) Always	3	11	0	0	3	23	0	0	10	37	3	27	5	39	2	67	
Seldom	3	11	1	9	2	15	0	0	7	26	4	36	2	15	1	33	
If cost is in line with possible loss or if forecast and forward rates differ	2	7	1	9	1	8	0	0	2	7	2	18	0	0	0	0	0 0

*There were no responses in the "Never" category.
**There were no responses in the "Not at all" category.

EXHIBIT 11: REGULARITY OF HEDGING TRANSLATION EXPOSURE

Frequency	As completely as possible								Partially								Not at all							
Degree	Total	%	U.S.	%	U.K.	%	Can.	%	Total	%	U.S.	%	U.K.	%	Can.	%	Total	%	U.S.	%	U.K.	%	Can.	%
(Almost) Always	4	15	2	18	2	15	0	0	4	15	3	27	1	8	0	0	3	11	0	0	2	15	1	33
Seldom	2	7	0	0	1	8	1	33	5	19	4	36	0	0	1	33	0	0	0	0	0	0	0	0
Never	0	0	0	0	0	0	0	0	0	0	0	0	0	0	0	0	8	30	1	9	7	54	0	0
If cost is in line with possible loss	1	4	1	9	0	0	0	0	0	0														

EXHIBIT 12: REASONS FOR HEDGING TRANSLATION EXPOSURE

	Respondents							
	Total	%	U.S.	%	U.K.	%	Can.	%
To reduce forex losses (EPS)	8	30	8	73	0	0	0	0
To reduce earnings volatility and forex translation losses	1	4	1	9	0	0	0	0
To reduce exposure due to funding of monetary assets in foreign currency	1	4	1	9	0	0	0	0
To avoid deliterious balance sheet ratios	1	4	0	0	1	8	0	0
To match liability and asset currencies	2	7	0	0	2	15	0	0
To reduce equity fluctuations	1	4	0	0	1	8	0	0
To reduce balance sheet exposure	1	4	0	0	1	8	0	0
To hedge foreign borrowings of parent company	1	4	0	0	0	0	1	33
To reduce part of transaction exposure	1	4	0	0	0	0	1	33
Not applicable	1	4	0	0	1	8	0	0
No response	9	33	1	9	7	54	1	33
	27	100	11	100	13	100	3	100

EXHIBIT 13: CHOICES OF SHORT-TERM HEDGING VEHICLE

	Respondents							
	Total	%	U.S.	%	U.K.	%	Can.	%
(a) Forward markets	16	59	6	55	7	54	3	100
(b) Money markets	1	4	1	9	0	0	0	0
(c) Overseas finance companies and other invoicing vehicles	0	0	0	0	0	0	0	0
(d) Other								
(a) and (b)	8	30	3	27	5	39	0	0
(a), (b) and (c)	1	4	1	9	0	0	0	0
Not applicable	1	4	0	0	1	8	0	0
	27	100	11	100	13	100	3	100

EXHIBIT 14:   METHODS OF EVALUATING LONG-TERM HEDGING STRATEGIES

	Respondents							
	Total	%	U.S.	%	U.K.	%	Can.	%
(a) Adjust the capitalization of overseas subsidiaries	0	0	0	0	0	0	0	0
(b) Evaluate alternative local vs. parent company currency-financing schemes	8	30	3	27	5	39	0	0
(c) Rely on exchange-rate forecasts to compare alternative financing schemes	3	11	0	0	2	15	1	33
(d) Other								
(a) and (b)	5	19	2	18	1	8	2	67
(a), (b) and (c)	2	7	2	18	0	0	0	0
(b) and (c)	4	15	2	18	2	15	0	0
Forex risk part of overall project evaluations	1	4	1	9	0	0	0	0
Not applicable	3	11	1	9	2	15	0	0
No response	1	4	0	0	1	8	0	0
	27	100	11	100	13	100	3	100

EXHIBIT 15:   TECHNIQUES TO EFFECT LONG-TERM HEDGING

	Respondents							
	Total	%	U.S.	%	U.K.	%	Can.	%
(a) Foreign currency-denominated debt instruments	9	33	2	18	5	39	2	67
(b) Parallel, swap or back-to-back loans	1	4	1	9	0	0	0	0
(c) Long-term forward contracts	0	0	0	0	0	0	0	0
(d) Other								
(a) and (b)	5	19	2	18	3	23	0	0
(a), (b) and (c)	3	11	0	0	3	23	0	0
(a) and (c)	6	22	4	36	1	8	1	33
None	2	7	2	18	0	0	0	0
Not applicable	1	4	0	0	1	8	0	0
	27	100	11	100	13	100	3	100

EXHIBIT 16: DECISIONMAKING RESPONSIBILITY IN THE EXCHANGE-RATE REALM

(a) For General Policy Formation

	Respondents							
	Total	%	U.S.	%	U.K.	%	Can.	%
Treasurer and/or senior V.P. of finance	6	22	2	18	2	15	2	67
Headquarters	5	19	3	27	2	15	0	0
Senior corporation management	8	30	3	27	4	31	1	33
Treasury department	2	7	1	9	1	8	0	0
Department heads of treasury and asset and liability management	1	4	1	9	0	0	0	0
Committee of senior financial personnel	3	11	1	9	2	15	0	0
Directors	2	7	0	0	2	15	0	0
	27	100	11	100	13	100	3	100

(b) (1) For Analysis of Internal and External Data

	Respondents							
	Total	%	U.S.	%	U.K.	%	Can.	%
Treasurer	5	19	1	9	3	23	1	33
Assistant treasurer	1	4	1	9	0	0	0	0
Headquarters	1	4	0	0	1	8	0	0
Headquarters and affiliates	4	15	3	27	1	8	0	0
Subsidiaries	1	4	1	9	0	0	0	0
Senior management	1	4	1	9	0	0	0	0
Management	1	4	0	0	1	8	0	0
Corporate treasury	4	15	1	9	2	15	1	33
Forex exposure committee	1	4	1	9	0	0	0	0
Economics department	2	7	1	9	1	8	0	0
Geographic and cashier divisions	1	4	1	9	0	0	0	0
Manager, corporate cash resources	1	4	0	0	0	0	1	33
Finance director	1	4	0	0	1	8	0	0
Headquarters financial staff	2	7	0	0	2	15	0	0
To be developed	1	4	0	0	1	8	0	0
	27	100	11	100	13	100	3	100

EXHIBIT 16 continued

(b) (2) For Development of Forecasts

	Respondents							
	Total	%	U.S.	%	U.K.	%	Can.	%
Treasurer	3	11	1	9	2	15	0	0
Assistant treasurer	1	4	1	9	0	0	0	0
Headquarters and affiliates	4	15	3	27	1	8	0	0
Subsidiaries	2	7	1	9	1	8	0	0
Senior management	1	4	1	9	0	0	0	0
Treasury and corporate planning departments	1	4	0	0	1	8	0	0
Group treasury	1	4	0	0	1	8	0	0
Economics department	2	7	1	9	1	8	0	0
Economics, world banking and cashier departments	1	4	1	9	0	0	0	0
Manager, corporate cash resources	1	4	0	0	0	0	1	33
Manager, financial operations	1	4	0	0	0	0	1	33
Financial staff	4	15	1	9	2	15	1	33
Normal management structure	1	4	0	0	1	8	0	0
External sources	1	4	1	9	0	0	0	0
To be developed	1	4	0	0	1	8	0	0
No response	2	7	0	0	2	15	0	0
	27	100	11	100	13	100	3	100

(c) For Deciding Which Exposures to Hedge

	Respondents							
	Total	%	U.S.	%	U.K.	%	Can.	%
Treasurer	3	11	1	9	2	15	0	0
Assistant treasurer	1	4	1	9	0	0	0	0
Headquarters	2	7	2	18	0	0	0	0
Subsidiaries	1	4	0	0	1	8	0	0
Senior financial management	3	11	1	9	0	0	2	67
Senior management and senior financial officers	3	11	2	18	1	8	0	0
Corporate treasury department	4	15	2	18	2	15	0	0
Corporate staffs and affiliates	3	11	1	9	2	15	0	0
Forex exposure management committee	2	7	1	9	1	8	0	0
Manager, corporate cash resources, and treasurer	1	4	0	0	0	0	1	33
Finance director	1	4	0	0	1	8	0	0
Finance division and subsidiaries	1	4	0	0	1	8	0	0
Senior executives	1	4	0	0	1	8	0	0
To be developed	1	4	0	0	1	8	0	0
	27	100	11	100	13	100	3	100

EXHIBIT 16 continued

(d) For Development and Implementation of Hedging Policies in Light of (c)

	Respondents							
	Total	%	U.S.	%	U.K.	%	Can.	%
Treasurer and assistant treasurer	1	4	1	9	0	0	0	0
Vice president-treasurer and assistant treasurer	1	4	0	0	0	0	1	33
Headquarters and subsidiaries	6	22	2	18	3	23	1	33
Subsidiaries	7	26	3	27	4	31	0	0
Senior financial management	1	4	1	9	0	0	0	0
Senior financial management and staff	1	4	1	9	0	0	0	0
Corporate treasury	3	11	2	18	1	8	0	0
Forex exposure management committee	1	4	1	9	0	0	0	0
Manager, corporate cash resources	1	4	0	0	0	0	1	33
Financial controller	1	4	0	0	1	8	0	0
Finance director	1	4	0	0	1	8	0	0
To be developed	1	4	0	0	1	8	0	0
No response	2	7	0	0	2	15	0	0
	27	100	11	100	13	100	3	100

EXHIBIT 17: CHANGES IN FOREIGN CURRENCY-DENOMINATED INVENTORIES

	Respondents							
	Total	%	U.S.	%	U.K.	%	Can.	%
None	17	63	6	55	8	62	3	100
Not significant	3	11	2	18	1	8	0	0
Not applicable	7	26	3	27	4	31	0	0
	27	100	11	100	13	100	3	100

EXHIBIT 18: EFFECTS OF FOREX RATE FLEXIBILITY ON INVENTORY MANAGEMENT

	Respondents							
	Total	%	U.S.	%	U.K.	%	Can.	%
None	12	44	4	36	7	54	1	33
Not significant	6	22	2	18	3	23	1	33
Longer holding of foreign-denominated inventories	1	4	1	9	0	0	0	0
Increase in awareness of forex rate fluctuation effects on inventory losses	1	4	1	9	0	0	0	0
Tighter inventory control	1	4	0	0	0	0	1	33
Not applicable	6	22	3	27	3	23	0	0
	27	100	11	100	13	100	3	100

EXHIBIT 19: CHANGES IN THE FOREIGN INVESTMENT/FOREIGN ASSET ACQUISITION DECISION DUE TO FLOATING FOREX RATES

	Respondents							
	Total	%	U.S.	%	U.K.	%	Can.	%
None	7	26	2	18	5	39	0	0
Not significant	8	30	2	18	4	31	2	67
Inclusion of forex exposure in analyses and increase in D.C.F rate	1	4	0	0	0	0	1	33
Consideration of translation risk implications	1	4	1	9	0	0	0	0
More consideration of risk of fluctuating forex rates	6	22	4	36	2	15	0	0
Minimization of investment levels	1	4	1	9	0	0	0	0
Addition of forex and inflation forecasts	1	4	0	0	1	8	0	0
Not applicable	2	7	1	9	1	8	0	0
	27	100	11	100	13	100	3	100

EXHIBIT 20: INDUSTRIES REPRESENTED BY RESPONDENTS

	Respondents							
	Total	%	U.S.	%	U.K.	%	Can.	%
Banking (financial services)	6	22	3	27	3	23	0	0
Chemical	1	4	1	9	0	0	0	0
Cosmetics	1	4	0	0	1	8	0	0
Electronics	2	7	2	18	0	0	0	0
Food and chemical	1	4	0	0	1	8	0	0
Industrial equipment	4	15	3	27	1	8	0	0
Information processing	1	4	1	9	0	0	0	0
Metal working (and wire)	2	7	0	0	1	8	1	33
Mining and natural resources	3	11	0	0	2	15	1	33
Packaging	1	4	0	0	1	8	0	0
Petroleum	4	15	1	9	2	15	1	33
Tobacco	1	4	0	0	1	8	0	0
	27	100	11	100	13	100	3	100

EXHIBIT 21: TOTAL SALES IN 1978
(Billions of Currency Units)

U.S. $	Respondents	%	U.K.£	Respondents	%
0.0– 0.3	2	18	0.0– 0.2	4	31
0.3– 0.7	1	9	0.2– 0.5	2	15
0.7– 1.0	1	9	0.5– 1.0	1	8
1.0– 3.0	2	18	1.0– 5.0	1	8
3.0–25.0	2	18	5.0–10.0	0	0
25.0–50.0	1	9	10.0–15.0	2	15
Over 50.0	1	9	Over 15.0	0	0
Not applicable	1	9	Not applicable	3	23
	11	100		13	100

	Can.$	Respondents	%
	1.0– 5.0	2	67
	5.0–10.0	1	33
		3	100

EXHIBIT 22: FOREIGN SALES AS A PERCENT OF TOTAL SALES, 1978

Percent	Total	%	U.S.	%	U.K.	%	Can.	%
					Respondents			
0-10	1	4	0	0	0	0	1	33
10-20	4	15	1	9	2	15	1	33
20-30	2	7	2	18	0	0	0	0
30-40	5	19	4	36	1	8	0	0
40-50	1	4	1	9	0	0	0	0
50-60	2	7	1	9	1	8	0	0
60-70	2	7	0	0	2	15	0	0
70-80	2	7	0	0	2	15	0	0
80-90	2	7	0	0	1	8	1	33
90 +	1	4	0	0	1	8	0	0
Not applicable	4	15	1	9	3	23	0	0
No response	1	4	1	9	0	0	0	0
	27	100	11	100	13	100	3	100

EXHIBIT 23: ASSETS
(Billions of Currency Units)

U.S. $	Respondents	%	U.K. £	Respondents	%
0.0- 0.3	2	18	0.0 - 0.1	3	23
0.3- 1.0	0	0	0.1 - 0.25	3	23
1.0- 3.0	3	27	0.25- 0.5	0	0
3.0- 6.0	2	18	0.5 - 0.75	1	8
6.0-10.0	0	0	0.75- 1.0	0	0
10.0-15.0	0	0	1.0 - 2.5	2	15
15.0-20.0	1	9	2.5 - 5.0	1	8
20.0-25.0	1	9	5.0 -10.0	1	8
25.0-40.0	0	0	10.0 -15.0	2	15
40.0-45.0	1	9	Over 15.0	0	0
Over 45.0	1	9			
	11	100		13	100

Can.$	Respondents	%
0.0-2.0	0	0
2.0-4.0	2	67
Over 4.0	1	33
	3	100

EXHIBIT 24: FOREIGN ASSETS AS A PERCENT OF TOTAL ASSETS

Percent	Respondents							
	Total	%	U.S.	%	U.K.	%	Can.	%
0-10	3	11	1	9	0	0	2	67
10-20	4	15	2	18	2	15	0	0
20-30	4	15	4	36	0	0	0	0
30-40	2	7	1	9	1	8	0	0
40-50	3	11	1	9	2	15	0	0
50-60	1	4	1	9	0	0	0	0
60-70	4	15	1	9	2	15	1	33
70-80	4	15	0	0	4	31	0	0
80-90	1	4	0	0	1	8	0	0
90-100	1	4	0	0	1	8	0	0
	27	100	11	100	13	100	3	100

EXHIBIT 25: RESPONDENTS' EXPOSURE IN FOREIGN CURRENCIES

	Total	%	U.S.	%	U.K.	%	Can.	%
Argentine peso	1	4	1	9	0	0	0	0
Australian dollar	9	33	5	46	3	23	1	33
Belgian franc	5	19	3	27	2	15	0	0
Brazilian cruzeiro	4	15	3	27	1	8	0	0
British pound	10	37	8	73	–	–	2	67
Canadian dollar	11	41	6	55	5	39	–	–
Columbian peso	1	4	1	9	0	0	0	0
Danish krone	1	4	0	0	1	8	0	0
Deutsche mark	13	48	7	64	6	46	0	0
Dutch guilden (florin)	3	11	0	0	3	23	0	0
French franc	11	41	7	64	4	31	0	0
Hong Kong dollar	3	11	3	27	0	0	0	0
Italian lira	8	30	7	64	1	8	0	0
Japanese yen	6	22	5	46	0	0	1	33
Mexican peso	3	11	3	27	0	0	0	0
Singapore dollar	1	4	1	9	0	0	0	0
S. African rand	4	15	2	18	2	15	0	0
Swedish krona	3	11	1	9	1	8	1	33
Swiss franc	7	26	5	46	2	15	0	0
Saudi riyal	1	4	0	0	1	8	0	0
Taiwan dollar	1	4	1	9	0	0	0	0
U.A.E. dirham	1	4	0	0	1	8	0	0
U.S. dollar	10	37	–	–	7	54	3	100
Spanish peseta	3	11	3	27	0	0	0	0
Most of the above currencies	4	15	1	9	3	23	0	0
Others (not specified)	2	7	1	9	1	8	0	0
No response	1	4	1	9	0	0	0	0

EXHIBIT 26: NUMBER OF COUNTRIES IN WHICH FIRMS HAVE PRODUCTIVE OPERATIONS

Number of Countries	Respondents							
	Total	%	U.S.	%	U.K.	%	Can.	%
1	2	7	1	9	0	0	1	33
2	1	4	0	0	0	0	1	33
3	0	0	0	0	0	0		
4	2	7	1	9	1	8		
5	0	0	0	0	0	0		
6	1	4	0	0	1	8		
7	2	7	1	9	1	8	0	0
8	2	7	1	9	1	8		
9	0	0	0	0	0	0		
10	1	4	0	0	1	8		
11–20	3	11	2	18	1	8		
21–30	4	15	1	9	2	15	1	33
31–50	1	4	1	9	0	0		
51–70	1	4	0	0	1	8		
71–80	3	11	1	9	2	15	0	0
81–100	0	0	0	0	0	0		
100+	2	7	1	9	1	8		
Not applicable	1	4	1	9	0	0		
No response	1	4	0	0	1	8	0	0
	27	100	11	100	13	100	3	100

EXHIBIT 27: NUMBER OF COUNTRIES IN WHICH FIRMS HAVE SALES

Number of Countries	Respondents							
	Total	%	U.S.	%	U.K.	%	Can.	%
1–10	3	11	1	9	1	8	1	33
11–20	2	7	0	0	2	15		
21–30	1	4	1	9	0	0		
31–50	2	7	0	0	2	15		
51–70	1	4	1	9	0	0	0	0
71–90	1	4	1	9	0	0		
91–110	2	7	1	9	1	8		
111–120	2	7	2	18	0	0		
120+	2	7	0	0	2	15		
"Widely"	1	4	0	0	0	0	1	33
"Most"	2	7	0	0	1	8	1	33
"All"	2	7	1	9	1	8	0	0
Not applicable/ available	4	15	1	9	3	23	0	0
No response	2	7	2	18	0	0	0	0
	27	100	11	100	13	100	3	100

EXHIBIT 28: NUMBER OF COUNTRIES IN WHICH FIRMS HAVE REVENUES

Number of Countries	Respondents							
	Total	%	U.S.	%	U.K.	%	Can.	%
1–10	3	11	1	9	1	8	1	33
11–20	3	11	0	0	3	23		
21–30	2	7	2	18	0	0		
31–50	4	15	2	18	2	15		
51–70	2	7	1	9	1	8	0	0
71–90	2	7	1	9	1	8		
91–100	1	4	0	0	1	8		
110 +	3	11	1	9	2	15		
"Widely"	1	4	0	0	0	0	1	33
"All"	1	4	0	0	1	8	0	0
Not applicable/ available	3	11	1	9	1	8	1	33
No response	2	7	2	18	0	0	0	0
	27	100	11	100	13	100	3	100

APPENDIX 3
Annualized Monthly Percentage Changes of Major Exchange Rates, 1972–80[1]

	U.S.$ against £	U.S.$ against DM	U.S.$ against Sw. Fr.	U.S.$ against Yen	£ against DM	£ against Sw. Fr.	£ against Yen	DM against Sw. Fr.	DM against Yen	Sw. Fr. against Yen
1972										
Jan.	− 5.5	− 10.5	− 1.7	− 24.5	− 5.3	4.0	− 20.1	9.9	− 15.6	− 23.2
Feb.	− 4.4	− 4.3	− 10.4	1.6	0.1	− 6.2	6.3	− 6.4	6.2	13.4
Mar.	2.2	4.6	10.0	0.6	2.3	7.7	− 1.5	5.2	− 3.8	− 8.6
Apr.	− 0.9	− 1.8	− 6.7	2.7	− 0.9	− 5.9	3.7	− 5.0	4.6	10.2
May	124.7	− 9.1	− 28.0	− 30.4	− 59.5	− 68.0	− 69.0	− 20.9	− 23.4	− 3.2
June	− 3.6	9.1	12.0	25.4	13.2	16.2	30.1	2.6	14.9	12.0
July	0.7	6.3	2.4	− 2.5	5.5	1.6	− 3.2	− 3.7	− 8.3	− 4.8
Aug.	15.1	4.9	6.5	2.6	− 8.8	− 7.5	− 10.8	1.5	− 2.2	− 3.6
Sept.	48.2	1.2	− 0.5	− 0.9	− 31.7	− 32.8	− 33.1	− 1.6	− 2.0	− 0.4
Oct.	− 5.3	− 4.6	− 6.9	− 0.4	0.8	− 1.7	5.2	− 2.5	4.4	7.0
Nov.	2.4	3.4	− 0.8	5.2	1.0	− 3.1	2.8	− 4.0	1.8	6.1
Dec.	− 15.8	− 16.0	− 39.5	− 3.1	− 0.2	− 28.1	15.1	− 28.0	15.3	60.2
1973										
Jan.	− 40.4	− 72.4	− 82.0	− 78.3	− 53.7	− 69.8	− 63.6	− 34.8	− 21.4	20.4
Feb.	2.7	− 2.0	43.4	− 1.0	− 4.6	39.6	− 3.6	46.3	1.1	− 30.9
Mar.	− 2.5	3.9	4.2	3.0	6.6	6.9	5.6	0.3	− 0.9	− 1.2
Apr.	− 31.5	− 45.9	− 44.7	− 5.4	− 21.0	− 19.3	38.1	2.2	74.8	71.0
May	− 7.0	− 71.9	− 49.2	− 11.8	− 69.8	− 45.4	− 5.2	80.8	214.1	73.7
June	38.4	− 40.4	− 30.5	5.7	− 57.0	− 49.8	− 23.6	16.7	77.5	52.0
July	30.1	98.8	126.0	10.4	52.8	73.7	− 15.2	13.7	− 44.5	− 51.2
Aug.	24.8	− 20.0	− 1.4	1.8	− 35.9	− 21.0	− 18.5	23.2	27.1	3.2
Sept.	− 11.9	16.0	32.5	4.2	31.6	50.4	18.2	14.2	− 10.2	− 21.4
Oct.	61.9	131.3	51.3	80.8	42.9	− 6.5	11.7	− 34.6	− 21.8	19.5
Nov.	10.7	43.7	15.2	− 0.9	29.8	4.1	− 10.5	− 19.8	− 31.0	− 14.0
Dec.	27.3	28.5	2.5	118.8	1.0	− 19.5	71.9	− 20.3	70.3	113.5
1974										
Jan.	− 13.9	− 32.0	− 37.0	− 35.3	− 21.0	− 26.8	− 24.9	− 7.3	− 4.9	2.6
Feb.	− 36.4	− 48.5	− 35.3	− 41.4	− 19.0	1.7	− 7.8	25.6	13.8	− 9.4
Mar.	− 17.5	− 34.5	− 33.7	18.1	− 20.6	− 19.6	43.2	1.2	80.2	78.0
Apr.	19.4	48.1	27.8	12.2	24.0	7.0	− 6.0	− 13.7	− 24.2	− 12.1
May	3.3	13.5	6.8	9.9	9.8	3.4	6.4	− 5.9	− 3.1	2.9
June	1.8	12.3	− 12.6	79.9	10.3	− 14.1	76.7	− 22.1	60.2	105.7
July	43.3	50.5	21.8	20.9	5.0	− 15.0	− 15.6	− 19.0	− 19.6	− 0.7
Aug.	− 7.9	− 4.3	− 21.2	− 16.9	4.0	− 14.4	− 9.8	− 17.7	− 13.2	5.4
Sept.	− 1.8	− 29.3	− 27.9	7.0	− 28.1	− 26.6	9.0	2.0	51.5	48.5
Oct.	5.6	− 38.8	− 49.5	0.3	− 42.0	− 52.2	− 5.0	− 17.6	63.8	98.7
Nov.	− 10.7	− 26.9	− 56.8	2.4	− 18.1	− 51.6	14.7	− 40.9	40.0	136.9
Dec.	− 16.5	− 30.0	− 14.8	− 9.9	− 16.2	2.0	7.9	21.7	28.7	5.8
1975										
Jan.	− 20.7	− 28.0	− 36.6	− 38.1	− 9.3	− 20.1	− 21.9	− 11.9	− 14.0	− 2.3
Feb.	13.8	49.6	92.0	26.1	31.4	68.7	10.9	28.4	− 15.7	− 34.3
Mar.	29.7	11.7	10.1	1.8	− 13.9	− 15.1	− 21.5	− 1.4	− 8.8	− 7.5
Apr.	20.0	− 15.8	− 23.7	− 4.5	− 29.8	− 36.4	− 20.5	− 9.4	13.3	25.1
May	94.0	7.0	1.4	18.9	− 44.8	− 47.8	− 38.7	− 5.3	11.1	17.3
June	23.5	180.2	147.7	9.4	126.9	100.6	− 11.4	− 11.6	− 61.0	− 55.8
July	27.2	5.7	− 5.5	0.5	− 17.0	− 25.8	− 21.0	− 10.6	− 4.9	6.4
Aug.	48.1	35.6	29.7	22.2	− 8.5	− 12.5	− 17.5	− 4.4	− 9.9	− 5.8
Sept.	− 18.7	− 33.5	− 42.2	− 4.2	− 18.3	− 29.0	17.8	− 13.1	44.1	65.8
Oct.	40.4	37.3	29.3	6.1	− 2.2	− 8.0	− 24.5	− 5.9	− 22.7	− 17.9
Nov.	− 1.9	− 2.7	− 23.3	6.6	− 0.8	− 21.8	8.6	− 21.2	9.6	39.0
Dec.	− 3.7	− 12.3	− 7.9	− 4.1	− 9.0	− 4.4	− 0.5	5.0	9.3	4.1
1976										
Jan.	2.7	− 9.0	− 13.5	− 5.9	− 11.3	− 15.8	− 8.4	− 5.0	3.3	8.7
Feb.	94.8	− 12.3	− 12.8	− 8.7	− 55.0	− 55.3	− 53.2	− 0.6	4.1	4.7
Mar.	62.0	− 2.7	− 11.1	− 1.8	− 39.9	− 45.1	− 39.4	− 8.7	0.9	10.4
Apr.	72.8	29.0	− 23.7	3.6	− 25.4	− 55.8	− 40.0	− 40.8	− 19.6	35.8
May	− 16.4	− 7.2	3.4	− 9.5	11.1	23.7	8.2	11.4	− 2.5	− 12.5
June	− 0.3	− 13.2	8.1	− 16.9	− 12.9	8.5	− 16.6	24.5	− 4.3	− 23.2
July	5.5	− 7.0	− 2.1	− 18.2	− 11.8	− 7.2	− 22.5	5.3	− 12.1	− 16.5
Aug.	125.6	− 36.3	− 15.2	− 4.6	− 71.8	− 62.4	− 57.7	33.2	49.9	12.5
Sept.	74.1	− 17.1	− 7.2	35.1	− 52.4	− 46.7	− 22.4	11.9	62.8	45.5
Oct.	− 38.9	4.0	8.0	10.0	70.2	76.8	80.1	3.9	5.8	1.9
Nov.	− 29.7	− 21.9	0.6	− 14.6	11.1	43.1	21.4	28.8	9.3	− 15.2
Dec.	− 8.9	28.8	35.4	− 17.3	41.4	48.7	− 9.2	5.2	− 35.8	− 38.9

[1] Data presented are based on the change to the 15th of the month indicated from the 15th of the previous month.

	U.S.$ against £	U.S.$ against DM	U.S.$ against Sw. Fr.	U.S.$ against Yen	£ against DM	£ against Sw. Fr.	£ against Yen	DM against Sw. Fr.	DM against Yen	Sw. Fr. against Yen
1977										
Jan.	0.8	− 9.0	24.9	− 21.6	− 9.7	23.9	− 22.2	37.2	− 13.8	− 37.2
Feb.	− 4.2	1.5	− 4.2	− 19.1	6.0	0.0	− 15.5	− 5.7	− 20.3	− 15.5
Mar.	0.4	− 17.7	− 14.3	0.4	− 18.0	− 14.7	0.0	4.1	22.0	17.2
Apr.	0.1	3.1	− 4.0	− 2.4	3.0	− 4.1	− 2.5	− 6.9	− 5.3	1.7
May	− 1.2	− 8.9	− 18.2	− 35.2	− 7.8	− 17.3	− 34.5	− 10.2	− 28.9	− 20.8
June	− 10.5	− 22.4	− 24.6	− 2.0	− 13.3	− 15.7	9.5	− 2.8	26.3	29.9
July	− 4.0	12.8	− 6.7	1.1	17.5	− 2.8	5.3	− 17.3	− 10.4	8.4
Aug.	− 3.2	− 2.5	− 21.6	− 13.8	0.8	− 19.0	− 11.0	− 19.6	− 11.7	9.8
Sept.	− 46.3	− 26.7	− 44.7	− 49.7	36.5	3.0	− 6.3	− 24.6	− 31.4	− 9.0
Oct.	16.7	− 14.3	− 31.3	− 21.7	− 26.5	− 41.1	− 32.9	− 19.9	− 8.7	14.0
Nov.	− 47.4	− 49.7	− 64.0	− 20.6	− 4.4	− 31.6	51.0	− 28.5	57.8	120.7
Dec.	− 18.5	6.2	− 4.7	11.0	30.4	16.9	36.3	− 10.3	4.5	16.5
1978										
Jan.	5.4	− 41.6	− 61.7	− 15.3	− 44.6	− 63.7	− 19.6	− 34.5	45.1	121.4
Feb.	64.1	− 5.9	2.1	− 59.6	− 42.7	− 37.8	− 75.4	8.6	− 57.0	− 60.4
Mar.	28.5	48.3	97.9	19.4	15.4	54.0	− 7.0	33.4	− 19.5	− 39.7
Apr.	− 5.4	10.7	− 23.7	− 13.4	17.1	− 19.3	− 8.5	− 31.0	− 21.8	13.4
May	− 16.1	− 10.7	− 25.1	− 63.8	6.4	− 10.7	− 56.9	− 16.1	− 59.5	− 51.7
June	− 36.4	− 18.0	− 53.7	− 60.2	28.9	− 27.3	− 37.4	− 43.6	− 51.4	− 13.9
July	− 7.2	− 25.7	− 48.9	11.1	− 20.0	− 44.9	19.7	− 31.2	49.6	117.4
Aug.	− 18.3	− 26.2	− 49.5	− 7.0	− 9.6	− 38.1	13.8	− 31.5	25.9	83.9
Sept.	− 44.2	− 69.9	− 34.2	− 47.7	− 46.1	18.0	− 6.2	119.0	74.0	− 20.5
Oct.	108.8	198.5	433.6	210.5	42.9	155.5	48.7	78.8	4.0	− 41.8
Nov.	− 41.8	− 48.0	− 51.8	− 15.8	− 10.6	− 17.2	44.6	− 7.4	61.8	74.7
Dec.	35.9	41.5	81.1	65.2	4.1	33.2	21.6	28.0	16.7	− 8.8
1979										
Jan.	− 18.2	− 12.0	− 20.3	0.6	7.5	− 2.6	23.0	− 9.4	14.4	26.3
Feb.	− 22.1	11.1	20.5	52.1	42.6	54.7	95.2	8.5	36.9	26.2
Mar.	6.6	17.0	15.1	73.7	9.7	8.0	62.9	− 1.6	48.5	50.9
Apr.	− 8.1	10.4	7.0	3.5	20.2	16.4	12.6	− 3.1	− 6.3	− 3.3
May	− 46.4	− 36.8	− 38.8	− 13.7	18.0	14.3	61.2	− 3.2	36.5	41.0
June	− 51.3	− 11.3	− 8.3	− 12.9	82.0	88.0	78.6	3.3	− 1.8	− 5.0
July	38.5	4.6	10.0	32.0	− 24.5	− 20.6	− 4.7	5.1	26.2	20.0
Aug.	30.9	− 43.6	− 54.2	25.5	− 56.9	− 65.0	− 4.2	− 18.8	122.4	173.7
Sept.	103.4	53.5	125.8	99.7	− 24.5	11.1	− 1.8	47.1	30.1	− 11.6
Oct.	− 50.0	− 39.5	− 36.9	79.6	21.0	26.2	259.3	4.3	196.9	184.7
Nov.	− 10.5	− 4.0	− 3.4	− 38.3	7.3	8.0	− 31.1	0.6	− 35.8	− 36.1
Dec.	− 20.1	9.6	23.1	− 1.8	37.3	54.2	23.0	12.3	− 10.4	− 20.2
1980										
Jan.	− 5.7	30.4	78.3	82.1	38.2	89.0	93.0	36.8	39.6	2.1
Feb.	80.4	208.6	174.2	− 7.6	71.1	52.0	− 48.8	− 11.2	− 70.1	− 66.3
Mar.	− 40.1	− 62.1	− 71.7	− 41.4	− 36.6	− 52.7	− 2.2	− 25.4	54.3	106.9
Apr.	− 40.7	− 16.5	− 13.6	− 55.7	40.7	45.7	− 25.4	3.5	− 47.0	− 48.8
May	1.3	− 7.1	− 12.6	− 18.1	− 8.3	− 13.7	− 19.1	− 6.0	− 11.9	− 6.3
June	4.2	10.3	14.4	49.2	5.9	9.8	43.3	3.7	35.3	30.5
July	− 19.4	17.3	12.1	− 32.7	45.5	39.0	− 16.6	− 4.5	− 42.7	− 40.0
Aug.	0.3	8.2	− 5.6	− 34.0	7.9	− 5.9	− 34.2	− 12.8	− 39.0	− 30.1
Sept.	− 22.4	60.3	35.3	− 11.7	106.5	74.3	13.8	− 15.6	− 44.9	− 34.7
Oct.	44.3	24.9	28.5	42.6	− 13.4	− 11.0	− 1.2	2.8	14.2	11.0
Nov.	− 11.0	29.8	36.1	− 52.9	45.7	52.8	− 47.1	4.9	− 63.8	− 65.4
Dec.	12.3	102.9	103.0	20.3	179.0	83.6	1.0	− 1.0	81.2	− 175.8

Source: National Westminster Bank Ltd.

Members of the
British-North American Committee

SILAS S. CATHCART
Chairman and Chief Executive Officer,
Illinois Tool Works, Inc., Chicago, Illinois

HAROLD VAN B. CLEVELAND
Vice President, Citibank, N.A., New York,
N.Y.

DONALD M. COX
Director and Senior Vice President, Exxon
Corporation, New York, N.Y.

FRANK J. CUMMISKEY
IBM Vice President and President,
General Business Group/International,
IBM Corporation, White Plains, New York

JAMES W. DAVANT
Chairman of the Board, Paine Webber
Incorporated, New York, N.Y.

RALPH P. DAVIDSON
Chairman, Time Incorporated, New York,
N.Y.

DIRK DE BRUYNE
Managing Director, Royal Dutch/Shell
Group of Companies, London

A.H.A. DIBBS
Deputy Chairman, National Westminster
Bank Limited, London

SIR RICHARD DOBSON
Richmond, Surrey

WILLIAM DODGE
Ottawa, Ontario

WILLIAM H. DONALDSON
Chairman and Chief Executive,
Donaldson Enterprises Inc., New York,
N.Y.

PETER P. DONIS
Executive Vice President, Caterpillar
Tractor Company, Peoria, Illinois

GEOFFREY DRAIN
General Secretary, National Association
of Local Government Officers, London

JOHN DU CANE
Director, AMAX, Ltd. (London), London

TERRY DUFFY
President, Amalgamated Union of
Engineering Workers, London

GERRY EASTWOOD
General Secretary, Association of Pattern-
makers and Allied Craftsmen, London

HARRY E. EKBLOM
Chairman and Chief Executive Officer,
European American Bancorp, New York,
N.Y.

MOSS EVANS
General Secretary, Transport and General
Workers' Union, London

J.K. FINLAYSON
President, The Royal Bank of Canada,
Toronto, Ontario

GLENN FLATEN
President, Canadian Federation of
Agriculture, Regina, Saskatchewan

*RICHARD W. FOXEN
Corporate Vice President-International,
Rockwell International Corp., Pittsburgh,
Pennsylvania

*SIR ALISTAIR FRAME
Deputy Chairman and Chief Executive,
Rio-Tinto Zinc Corporation, London

ROBERT R. FREDERICK
Executive Vice President, International
Sector, General Electric Company, Fair-
field, Connecticut

THEODORE GEIGER
Distinguished Research Professor of
Intersocietal Relations, School of Foreign
Service, Georgetown University,
Washington, D.C.

GWAIN GILLESPIE
Senior Vice President-Finance and
Administration, Heublein Inc., Farm-
ington, Connecticut

MALCOLM GLENN
Executive Vice President, Reed Holdings,
Incorporated, Rickmansworth, Herts.

GEORGE GOYDER
Sudbury, Suffolk

JOHN H. HALE
Executive Vice President, Alcan
Aluminium Limited, Montreal, Quebec

HON. HENRY HANKEY
British Secretary, BNAC, Westerham,
Kent

---

*Became a member of the Committee after the statement was circulated for signature.

AUGUSTIN S. HART, JR.
Director, Quaker Oats Company, Chicago, Illinois

FRED L. HARTLEY
Chairman and President, Union Oil Company of California, Los Angeles, California

G.R. HEFFERNAN
President, Co-Steel International Ltd., Whitby, Ontario

HENRY J. HEINZ II
Chairman of the Board, H.J. Heinz Company, Pittsburgh, Pennsylvania

ROBERT HENDERSON
Chairman, Kleinwort Benson Ltd., London

*TREVOR HOLDSWORTH
Chairman, Guest, Keen & Nettlefolds Ltd., London

HENDRIK S. HOUTHAKKER
Professor of Economics, Harvard University, Cambridge, Massachusetts

TOM JACKSON
General Secretary, Union of Communication Workers, London

DONALD P. JACOBS
Dean, J.L. Kellogg Graduate School of Management, Northwestern University, Evanston, Illinois

JOHN V. JAMES
Chairman of the Board, President and Chief Executive Officer, Dresser Industries, Inc., Dallas, Texas

GEORGE S. JOHNSTON
President, Scudder, Stevens & Clark, New York, N.Y..

JOSEPH D. KEENAN
President, Union Label and Service Trades Department, AFL-CIO, Washington, D.C.

CURTIS M. KLAERNER
President and Chief Operating Officer, Commonwealth Oil Refining Company, San Antonio, Texas

H.U.A. LAMBERT
Chairman, Barclays Bank International Ltd., London

HERBERT H. LANK
Honorary Director, Du Pont Canada Inc., Montreal, Quebec

*INGRAM LENTON
Managing Director, The Bowater Corporation Ltd., London

WILLIAM A. LIFFERS
Vice Chairman, American Cyanamid Company, Wayne, New Jersey

FRANKLIN A. LINDSAY
Chairman, Itek Corporation, Lexington, Massachusetts

SIR PETER MACADAM
Chairman, B.A.T. Industries Ltd., London

RAY W. MACDONALD
Honorary Chairman, Burroughs Corporation, Stuart, Florida

IAN MacGREGOR
Honorary Chairman, AMAX Inc., Greenwich, Connecticut

CARGILL MacMILLAN, JR.
Senior Vice President, Cargill Inc., Minneapolis, Minnesota

JOHN D. MACOMBER
Chairman, Celanese Corporation, New York, N.Y.

J.P. MANN
Deputy Chairman, United Biscuits (Holdings) Ltd., Isleworth, Middlesex

WILLIAM A. MARQUARD
Chairman, President and Chief Executive Officer, American Standard Inc., New York, N.Y.

A.B. MARSHALL
Chairman, Bestobell Ltd., London

WILLIAM J. McDONOUGH
Chairman, Asset and Liability Management Committee, The First National Bank of Chicago, Chicago, Illinois

DONALD E. MEADS
Chairman and President, Carver Associates, Plymouth Meeting, Pennsylvania

SIR PATRICK MEANEY
Group Managing Director, Thomas Tilling Limited, London

*Became a member of the Committee after the statement was circulated for signature.

C.J. MEDBERRY, III
Chairman of the Board, BankAmerica Corporation and Bank of America NT&SA, Los Angeles, California

SIR PETER MENZIES
Welwyn, Hertfordshire

JOHN MILLER
Vice Chairman and Acting President, NPA, Washington, D.C.

ALLEN E. MURRAY
President of Marketing and Refining Division, Mobil Oil Corporation, New York, N.Y.

KENNETH D. NADEN
President, National Council of Farmer Cooperatives, Washington, D.C.

CONOR CRUISE O'BRIEN
Director, Observer Newspaper Company, Ltd., London

WILLIAM S. OGDEN
Vice Chairman and Chief Financial Officer, The Chase Manhattan Bank, N.A., New York, N.Y.

PAUL L. PARKER
Executive Vice President, General Mills, Inc., Minneapolis, Minnesota

BROUGHTON PIPKIN
Stow-on-the-Wold, Gloucestershire

GEORGE J. POULIN
General Vice President, International Association of Machinists & Aerospace Workers, Washington, D.C.

SIR RICHARD POWELL
Hill Samuel Group Ltd., London

ALFRED POWIS
Chairman and President, Noranda Mines Limited, Toronto, Ontario

*PAUL E. PRICE
Senior Vice President-Finance, Quaker Oats Company, Chicago, Illinois

LOUIS PUTZE
Consultant, Rockwell International Corp., Pittsburgh, Pennsylvania

MERLE R. RAWSON
Chairman and Chief Executive Officer, The Hoover Company, North Canton, Ohio

CARL E. REICHARDT
President and Director, Wells Fargo Bank, San Francisco, California

*GRANT L. REUBER
Deputy Chairman, Bank of Montreal, Montreal, Quebec

BEN ROBERTS
Professor of Industrial Relations, London School of Economics, London

HAROLD B. ROSE
Group Economic Advisor, Barclays Bank Limited, London

DAVID SAINSBURY
Director of Finance, J. Sainsbury Ltd., London

WILLIAM SALOMON
Limited Partner and Honorary Member of the Executive Committee, Salomon Brothers, New York, N.Y.

A.C.I. SAMUEL
Handcross, Sussex

*HOWARD SAMUEL
President, Industrial Union Department, AFL-CIO, Washington, D.C.

NATHANIEL SAMUELS
Chairman, Advisory Board, Lehman Brothers Kuhn Leob Inc., and Chairman, Olivetti Corporation, New York, N.Y.

SIR FRANCIS SANDILANDS
Chairman, Commercial Union Assurance Company, Ltd., London

HON. MAURICE SAUVE
Executive Vice President, Administrative and Public Affairs, Consolidated-Bathurst Inc., Montreal, Quebec

PETER F. SCOTT
President, Provincial Insurance Company, Ltd., Kendal, Westmoreland

ROBERT C. SEAMANS, JR.
Massachusetts Institute of Technology, Cambridge, Massachusetts

---

*Became a member of the Committee after the statement was circulated for signature.

LORD SEEBOHM
Dedham, Essex

THE EARL OF SELKIRK
President, Royal Central Asian Society,
London

JACOB SHEINKMAN
Secretary-Treasurer, Amalgamated
Clothing & Textile Workers' Union, New
York, N.Y.

LORD SHERFIELD
Chairman, Raytheon Europe International
Company, London

R. MICHAEL SHIELDS
Managing Director, Associated
Newspapers Group Ltd., London

GEORGE L. SHINN
Chairman and Chief Executive Officer,
The First Boston Corporation, New York,
N.Y.

GORDON R. SIMPSON
Chairman, General Accident Fire and Life
Assurance Corporation Ltd., Perth,
Scotland

SIR ROY SISSON
Chairman, Smiths Industries Limited,
London

SIR LESLIE SMITH
Chairman, BOC International Ltd.,
London

E. NORMAN STAUB
Chairman and Chief Executive Officer,
The Northern Trust Company, Chicago,
Illinois

RALPH I. STRAUS
New York, N.Y.

SIR ROBERT TAYLOR
Deputy Chairman, Standard Chartered
Bank Ltd., London

J.C. TURNER
General President, International Union of
Operating Engineers, AFL-CIO,
Washington, D.C.

W.O. TWAITS
Toronto, Ontario

MARTHA REDFIELD WALLACE
Director, The Henry Luce Foundation
Inc., New York, N.Y.

GLENN E. WATTS
President, Communications Workers of
America, AFL-CIO, Washington, D.C.

VISCOUNT WEIR
Vice Chairman, The Weir Group Limited,
Cathcart, Scotland

FREDERICK B. WHITTEMORE
Managing Director, Morgan Stanley & Co.
Incorporated, New York, N.Y.

SIR ERNEST WOODROOFE
Former Chairman, Unilever Ltd.,
Guildford, Surrey

*CHARLES WOOTTON
Senior Director, Foreign and Domestic
Policy Analysis & Planning, Gulf Oil
Corporation, Pittsburgh, Pennsylvania

---

*Became a member of the Committee after the statement was circulated for signature.

Sponsoring Organizations

The British-North American Research Association was inaugurated in December 1969. Its primary purpose is to sponsor research on British-North American economic relations in association with the British-North American Committee. Publications of the British-North American Research Association as well as publications of the British-North American Committee are available from the Association's office, 1 Gough Square, London EC4A 3DE (Tel. 01–353–6371). The Association is recognized as a charity and is governed by a Council under the chairmanship of Sir Alastair Down.

NPA is an independent, private, nonprofit, nonpolitical organization that carries on research and policy formulation in the public interest. NPA was founded during the Great Depression of the 1930s when conflicts among the major economic groups—business, labor, agriculture—threatened to paralyze national decisionmaking on the critical issues confronting American society. It was dedicated to the task of getting these diverse groups to work together to narrow areas of controversy and broaden areas of agreement and to provide on specific problems concrete programs for action planned in the best traditions of a functioning democracy. Such democratic planning, NPA believes, involves the development of effective governmental and private policies and programs not only by official agencies but also through the independent initiative and cooperation of the main private-sector groups concerned. And, to preserve and strengthen American political and economic democracy, the necessary government actions have to be consistent with, and stimulate the support of, a dynamic private sector.

NPA brings together influential and knowledgeable leaders from business, labor, agriculture, and the applied and academic professions to serve on policy committees. These committees identify emerging problems confronting the nation at home and abroad and seek to develop and agree upon policies and programs for coping with them. The research and writing for these committees are provided by NPA's professional staff and, as required, by outside experts.

In addition, NPA's professional staff undertakes research designed to provide data and ideas for policy makers and planners in government and the private sector. These activities include the preparation on a regular basis of economic and demographic projections for the national economy, regions, states, metropolitan areas, and counties; research on national goals and priorities, productivity and economic growth, welfare and dependency problems, employment and manpower needs, energy and environmental questions, and other economic and social problems confronting American society; and analyses and forecasts of changing international realities and their implications for U.S. policies.

NPA publications, including those of the British-North American Committee, can be obtained from the Association's office, 1606 New Hampshire Avenue, N.W., Washington, D.C. 20009 (Tel. 202–265–7685).

The C.D. Howe Institute was established in 1973 by the merger of the C.D. Howe Memorial Foundation and the Private Planning Association of Canada. It is a nonprofit, nonpolitical organization seeking to contribute nonpartisan research findings and commentary on Canadian economic policy issues.

The guiding principle of the Institute is to conduct its research and analysis in a manner that is balanced in approach, professional in method and readable in style.

To ensure diversity in perspective, participation is encouraged from organized labor, business, agricultural associations, and the professions.

While its focus is national, the Institute recognizes that Canada is composed of regions, each of which may have a particular point of view on policy issues, unique interests and concerns, and different concepts of national priorities. The Institute also pursues involvement from both of Canada's major linguistic communities.

It is not the purpose of the Institute to promote consensus on policy issues, although on occasion that may be feasible. The primary function is to add to public understanding of issues by providing sound analysis reflecting objective treatment of diverse points of view.

Although governments and their departments are excluded from Institute membership, the staff of the Institute seeks to develop good working relationships with public officials for the purposes of better understanding the basis for government decisions and contributing effectively to public policy formulation.

A Board of Directors is responsible for the general administration of the Institute, while the immediate direction of the policies, program and staff is vested in the President. The function of the Board is to make independent research and publication possible under the most favorable conditions and not to control the conduct and conclusions of research activity.

W.J. Bennett is Chairman, Carl E. Beigie is President and Chief Executive Officer, and Wendy Dobson is Executive Director and Treasurer of the Institute. Other officers are Barbara Hodgins, Vice President, Western Division, and Romana Cap, Corporate Secretary.

The Institute's publications are available from its offices, Suite 2064, 1155 Metcalfe Street, Montreal, Quebec H3B 2X7 (Tel. 514-879-1254), and Suite 410, Mount Royal Village, 1550-8th Street, S.W., Calgary, Alberta T2R 1K1.

61,738